THE
Mixer
COOK
BOOK

Illustrated by A C McInnes

THE
Mixer
COOK
BOOK

by SONIA ALLISON

COLLINS LONDON and GLASGOW

Companion volume
FREEZER COOKBOOK

Cover photograph
by courtesy of Sunbeam Electric Ltd.

ISBN 0 00 435515 6

First published 1972
© Sonia Allison 1972
Printed in Great Britain
Collins Clear-Type Press

Contents

Hints on Using Mixers & Blenders

Blenders and mixers are worth their weight in gold. They save time. They save energy. In some cases, they save money as well. And because they reduce many arm-aching cooking jobs to a minimum, one is encouraged to try out more creative and imaginative dishes, knowing full well that they are not going to be any more time-consuming than some of the simpler, less involved ones. At the same time, because blenders and mixers chop, grind, purée, blend, beat, whip, rub in, and in some cases, knead, nearly all one's favourite recipes can be made with the help of these two kitchen aids.

Like all pieces of valuable electrical equipment, blenders and mixers respond to good care, and two rules should always be strictly observed. The first is to read through the manufacturer's hand-out or instruction booklet BEFORE using the machine; the second, NEVER to get the motor wet. And now some general rules which apply to both pieces of equipment.

Mixers

1. Do not run the mixer for longer than 5 minutes at a time.
2. Be guided by the manufacturer's instructions and use the right attachments and bowl for the type of mixture being mixed.
3. When creaming fat and sugar together, make sure the fat is softened first (but do not allow it to melt and become oily), as this prevents it from sticking to the beaters and sides of bowl. If time is short and the fat is hard, rinse the bowl and beaters with very hot water first as this helps to soften the fat.
4. To ensure that the ingredients are mixed properly, scrape down sides of bowl frequently with wooden spoon or spatula, *remembering to switch off the machine first*.
5. If mixtures are light and require whisking (sponges and meringue, for example), run the machine at high speed. For medium weight mixtures such as fat and sugar, run machine at medium speed. High speed would scatter the mixture all over the sides of the bowl and low speed might cause the machine to labour. For heavier types of mixing, such as rubbing in, use low speed only. As a guide, use low speed for heavy mixtures and small amounts; higher speeds for lighter mixtures and larger amounts.
6. In general, avoid over-mixing. This applies most particularly to rubbed-in mixtures and double cream. When rubbing fat into flour, run the machine just long enough for the ingredients to resemble fine bread-crumbs and *no more*. Where pastry is concerned, too much mixing will make it difficult to handle; where cakes are concerned, the end result could be disappointing. When beating cream, do so at low or medium speed, watching it carefully all the time, as cream very quickly turns to butter if over-beaten.

6

Blenders

1. Do not over-run the blender. After 45 to 60 seconds, switch off the machine, leave it for a few seconds and start it up again if necessary.
2. Do not pour boiling liquids into the blender. Allow them to cool slightly first.
3. If the blender seems to be labouring and straining, then the mixture may be too dry and heavy. If this is the case, stop the machine and add a little more liquid. Alternatively, if more liquid will spoil the recipe, stop the machine and, with a spoon or spatula, push the mixture down the sides of the blender on to the cutting blades. Re-start the machine and continue blending, switching machine on and off at intervals.
4. Avoid over-filling the blender, or liquid may be forced up through the lid when the motor is running at full speed. A half-full blender works best, so if you have a large quantity of, for example, vegetables and liquid to purée, do it in two or three batches. Scrape down mixture from sides of blender after a few seconds with a wooden spoon or spatula, *remembering to switch off the machine first.* Re-start and continue to blend.
5. When grinding dry foods such as bread, large nuts, chocolate, and cheese, cut them into small cubes or slices before putting them into the machine. Large pieces frequently get caught under the cutting blades and the machine jams as a result. Another point here: when grinding dry foods, run the machine at low speed, and switch it on and off (rather than allow it to run continuously) to prevent it from labouring too much.
6. ALWAYS cover the machine with its own lid before starting the motor. A hand held on the lid is advisable as it helps to keep the blender steady.
7. NEVER put fingers into the blender while it is running.
8. If a grinding attachment is available use it, instead of the blender, for grinding up dry foods such as the ones previously mentioned, as well as for coffee beans, biscuits, cereals and crisps.

Care of Mixers & Blenders

1. Follow manufacturer's instructions regarding maintenance and *never* operate a faulty machine.
2. Wash washable parts in warm to hot detergent water, avoiding the use of abrasives, powerful detergent powders, washing soda, and bleaches.
3. Wipe wipeable parts with a cloth wrung out in hot detergent water, then dry with a tea towel.
4. The inside of the blender goblet may be cleaned easily by half-filling it with hot water, adding one or two squeezes of liquid detergent and then running the machine for a few seconds. Afterwards rinse and wipe dry. Alternatively, clean inside of blender with hot detergent water and a soft brush.
5. It is inadvisable to wash the blender in a washing-up machine.

CHAPTER 1
Soups & Starters

Soup-making becomes child's play with a blender, and in a matter of seconds you can whizz up delicious-tasting and luxury-smooth soups ranging from the familiar Tomato and Mushroom to exotics—like Gazpacho and Avocado Cream—from overseas.

Starters, often a problem, are solved for you in this section and there is a good choice of world-wide specialities including Greek Taramasalata, Italian Gnocchi, French-style Quiche and Mexican Quacamole.

Soups

SPEEDY GAZPACHO.
Serves 4 to 6

2 oz (50 gm) white bread, diced
1 medium green pepper
½ medium cucumber
1 medium onion
2 large tomatoes, skinned
1 teacup parsley
1 garlic clove
4 tablespoons olive oil
Juice of 1 medium lemon
1 to 2 level teaspoons salt
1 level teaspoon granulated sugar
1 can (¾ pint or 375 ml) tomato
   juice
Freshly milled black pepper to
   taste

1. Put bread dice, a few at a time, into blender. Run machine until bread is reduced to fine crumbs. Transfer to large bowl.
2. De-seed green pepper and cut into strips.
3. Peel cucumber and slice.
4. Slice onion and quarter tomatoes.
5. Put green pepper, cucumber, onion, tomatoes, parsley, garlic, oil, lemon juice, salt, sugar, and half the tomato juice into blender.
6. Run machine until ingredients are finely chopped.
7. Pour on to breadcrumbs with remaining tomato juice.
8. Mix thoroughly and season to taste with black pepper.
9. Cover and chill thoroughly.
10. Stir well before serving.

TOMATO SOUP
Serves 4

2 oz (50 gm) streaky bacon
1 lb (½ kilo) tomatoes, skinned
2 medium celery stalks
1 large onion
½ pint (250 ml) water
1 level dessertspoon cornflour
1 level teaspoon granulated sugar

1 teaspoon Worcestershire sauce
1 level teaspoon salt
1 or 2 grindings of black pepper
4 tablespoons single cream

1. Chop bacon coarsely and fry gently in its own fat until tender.
2. Quarter tomatoes. Break celery into 6 pieces. Slice onion.
3. Put vegetables into blender with bacon (and any fat from pan), half the water, cornflour, sugar, Worcestershire sauce, salt, and black pepper.
4. Blend until smooth.
5. Pour into pan and add remaining water.
6. Slowly bring to boil, stirring continuously.
7. Simmer 2 minutes over low heat.
8. Remove from heat; stir in cream.

MUSHROOM SOUP
Serves 4

12 oz (300 gm) washed and peeled
   mushrooms and stalks
1½ oz (37 gm) butter or margarine
1 pint (approximately ½ litre) cold
   milk
1 oz (25 gm) flour
1 level teaspoon salt
Pepper to taste
Grated nutmeg

1. Slice mushrooms and stalks thinly.
2. Heat butter or margarine in saucepan. Add mushroom slices and stalks, and fry gently for 5 minutes.
3. Meanwhile, pour all remaining ingredients, except nutmeg, into blender.
4. Run machine until mixture is smooth.
5. Add to mushrooms in saucepan.
6. Cook, stirring continuously, until soup comes to boil and thickens.
7. Simmer 5 minutes, then pour into 4 warm soup bowls.
8. Sprinkle top of each with nutmeg.

9

CREAM OF AVOCADO SOUP

Serves 4

1 oz (25 gm) butter or margarine
1 medium ripe avocado
1 pint ($\frac{1}{2}$ litre) milk
1 oz (25 gm) flour
$\frac{1}{2}$ level teaspoon dry mustard
1 level teaspoon onion salt
White pepper to taste
Juice of $\frac{1}{2}$ lemon
Curry powder

1. Melt butter in saucepan.
2. Halve avocado and scoop flesh into blender.
3. Add half the milk, flour, mustard, onion salt, and pepper to taste.
4. Blend until smooth. Pour into saucepan. Add rest of milk.
5. Cook, stirring continuously, until soup comes to the boil and thickens.
6. Simmer 2 minutes over low heat.
7. Remove from heat and stir in lemon juice.
8. Pour into 4 warm soup bowls and sprinkle top of each with curry powder.

CONTINENTAL FRUIT SOUP

Serves 4

4 oz (100 gm) strawberries
4 oz (100 gm) raspberries
4 oz (100 gm) stoned cherries (weighed after stoning)
$\frac{1}{2}$ pint (250 ml) water
4 oz (100 gm) granulated sugar
Rind of 1 small lemon, cut into strips
1 level tablespoon cornflour
6 heaped teaspoons soured cream
Powdered cinnamon

1. Put fruit into saucepan with water. Slowly bring to boil.
2. Add sugar and stir until dissolved.
3. Add lemon rind, cover pan, and lower heat.
4. Simmer gently for 15 minutes.
5. Remove strips of lemon rind.
6. Pour half the fruit mixture into blender. Add cornflour. Blend until smooth. Pour into saucepan.
7. Blend remaining fruit mixture until smooth and add to saucepan.
8. Cook, stirring continuously, until mixture comes to the boil and thickens.
9. Simmer 5 minutes.
10. Transfer to 4 soup bowls and chill thoroughly.
11. Before serving, top with soured cream and sprinkle with cinnamon.

HAM AND SWEET CORN CHOWDER

Serves 4

1 medium onion
1$\frac{1}{2}$ oz (37 gm) butter or margarine
1$\frac{1}{2}$ oz (37 gm) flour
1 pint (approximately $\frac{1}{2}$ litre) milk
$\frac{1}{2}$ teacup parsley
8 oz (200 gm) cold boiled potatoes, diced
3 oz (75 gm) cold boiled bacon, diced
4 heaped tablespoons cooked sweet corn
Salt and pepper to taste

1. Slice onion and put into blender.
2. Run machine until onion is fairly finely chopped.
3. Melt butter or margarine in saucepan. Add onion and fry slowly until pale gold.
4. Meanwhile, put flour, milk, and parsley into blender.
5. Run machine until ingredients are smooth and parsley is finely chopped.
6. Pour into saucepan. Cook, stirring continuously, until mixture comes to the boil and thickens.
7. Add all remaining ingredients.
8. Cover pan and simmer gently for 10 to 12 minutes, stirring occasionally.
9. Remove from heat and serve hot.

Starters

CHEESE AND HAM QUICHE

Serves 4 to 6

4 oz (100 gm) Short Crust Pastry
  (page 63)
2 oz (50 gm) lean ham
¼ pint (125 ml) single cream
2 standard eggs
½ level teaspoon salt
Pinch of nutmeg
1 level tablespoon grated
  Parmesan cheese
Watercress for garnishing

1. Pre-heat oven to hot, 450°F or Gas
   No. 8 (232°C).
2. Roll out pastry, and use to line a
   7 inch (17.5 cm) flan ring standing
   on a lightly greased baking tray.
3. Cut ham into thin strips and arrange
   over base of flan.
4. Put cream, eggs, salt, and nutmeg
   into blender. Blend until smooth.
5. Pour into flan case over ham.
6. Sprinkle top with cheese.
7. Put into centre of oven and at once
   reduce temperature to warm,
   325°F or Gas No. 3 (163°C).
8. Cook 30 to 40 minutes, or until
   filling is set.
9. Serve hot or cold.

TARAMASALATA

Greek style fish pâté
Serves 4 to 6

6 large slices white bread
6 oz (150 gm) smoked cod's roe
2 garlic cloves
1 small onion, sliced
¼ pint (125 ml) salad oil
4 tablespoons lemon juice
Freshly milled black pepper

1. Cut crusts off bread and discard.
2. Cut bread into large cubes and
   cover with hot water.
3. Soak a minute or two and squeeze
   dry.
4. Put into blender.
5. Spoon cod's roe away from skin
   and add to blender with all remaining ingredients except pepper.
6. With machine at low speed, blend
   until smooth.
7. Remove from blender and season to
   taste with freshly milled pepper.
8. Mound equal amounts on to 4 or 6
   individual plates and serve with
   freshly made toast.

STUFFED MUSHROOMS

Serves 4

8 large flat mushrooms
2 oz (50 gm) white bread, cubed
1 small onion, sliced
1 small celery stalk, broken into
  4 pieces
2 tablespoons hot milk
1 tablespoon canned or tubed
  tomato purée
Salt and pepper to taste
½ oz (12 gm) butter or margarine
Parsley for garnishing

1. Pre-heat oven to fairly hot, 400°F
   or Gas No. 6 (204°C).
2. Remove stalks from mushrooms,
   wash and dry.
3. Peel mushrooms, wash and pat dry
   with paper towels. Stand on buttered baking tray.
4. Put bread cubes, a few at a time,
   into blender. Run machine until
   bread is reduced to fine crumbs.
   Put into bowl.
5. Put onion and celery into blender.
   Run machine until ingredients are
   finely chopped.
6. Add to crumbs with milk, purée, and
   salt and pepper to taste.
7. Mix thoroughly, then pile equal
   amounts on top of mushrooms.
8. Dot with flakes of butter, then top
   each with a mushroom stalk.
9. Cook in centre of oven for 12 to 15
   minutes.
10. Garnish with parsley and serve
    straight away.

POTATO GNOCCHI

Serves 4

8 oz (200 gm) potatoes
1½ oz (37 gm) flour
1 standard egg, beaten
Salt and pepper to taste

TOPPING

About 1½ oz (37 gm) melted butter
Grated Parmesan cheese

1. Cook potatoes in boiling salted water until tender.
2. Drain and put into mixer bowl.
3. Break up with fork.
4. Add flour and egg.
5. With mixer at low speed, beat potatoes with beaters until smooth.
6. Season well to taste with salt and pepper.
7. Leave until completely cold.
8. Drop teaspoons of mixture into a pan of gently simmering salted water.
9. Cook until Gnocchi float to the top and are lightly puffed.
10. Remove from pan with a perforated spoon and transfer to 4 warm plates.
11. Coat with melted butter, then sprinkle with Parmesan cheese.
12. Serve straight away.

SPAGHETTI PIZZAIOLA

Serves 4

8 oz (200 gm) spaghetti
1½ lb (approximately ¾ kilo) ripe tomatoes
2 garlic cloves, peeled
1 teacup parsley
1 tablespoon salad oil
1 level teaspoon dried basil
1 level teaspoon salt
2 level teaspoons granulated sugar
3 or 4 grindings of black pepper
Grated Parmesan cheese

1. Cook spaghetti as directed on the packet.
2. Meanwhile, put tomatoes into large bowl and cover with boiling water. Leave 2 minutes. Drain and cover with cold water.
3. Drain again and slide off skins. Cut tomatoes into quarters.
4. Put half the tomatoes into blender with all remaining ingredients except cheese. Blend until smooth. Pour into saucepan. Repeat with rest of tomatoes. Add to saucepan.
5. Slowly bring to boil, stirring.
6. Lower heat and cover. Simmer 10 minutes.
7. Drain spaghetti thoroughly and, if liked, toss with a little butter or oil.
8. Transfer to 4 individual warm plates.
9. Top with sauce.
10. Hand Parmesan cheese separately.

CHICORY À LA GRECQUE

Serves 4

4 medium heads of chicory
1 dessertspoon lemon juice
¼ pint (125 ml) Blender or Mixer Mayonnaise (page 36)
½ teacup parsley
1 hard-boiled egg, quartered
1 dozen black olives
1 can red pimiento caps, cut into strips

1. Cut a thin slice off the base of each head of chicory, then remove core with a potato peeler.
2. Strip off any brown or damaged outer leaves. Wash chicory under cold running water.
3. Put into saucepan of gently boiling water to which the dessertspoon of lemon juice has been added.
4. Lower heat, cover pan, and cook gently for 20 minutes.
5. Drain thoroughly and leave until cold.
6. Put mayonnaise into blender with parsley.
7. Run machine until parsley is finely chopped. Stop machine.
8. Add egg and run machine until finely chopped.
9. Put chicory on to 4 individual plates.
10. Coat with mayonnaise mixture, then garnish with olives and pepper strips.

MEXICAN QUACAMOLE

Serves 4

1 tablespoon wine vinegar
1 tablespoon lemon juice

12

1 small garlic clove
1 small onion, sliced
1 small green pepper, de-seeded
  and cut into squares
1 level teaspoon salt
½ teacup parsley
3 tablespoons corn oil
2 medium ripe avocados
Freshly milled black pepper to
  taste

1. Put vinegar, lemon juice, garlic clove, onion, green pepper, salt, parsley and oil into blender.
2. Run machine at low speed until ingredients are finely chopped.
3. Halve avocados and scoop flesh into a bowl with a teaspoon.
4. Mash coarsely, then stir in blended ingredients.
5. Season to taste with pepper, then pile back into avocado shells.
6. Serve straight away.

EASY LIVER PÂTÉ

Serves 4

1 large onion, sliced
2 oz (50 gm) butter or margarine
12 oz (300 gm) chicken livers
2 tablespoons dry white wine
1 tablespoon lemon juice
2 tablespoons double cream
1 level teaspoon salt
1 heaped tablespoon parsley
3 hard-boiled eggs
Freshly milled black pepper to
  taste

1. Put onion into blender and run machine until finely chopped.
2. Heat butter or margarine in saucepan. Add onion and fry slowly until just beginning to turn golden.
3. Wash and dry livers.
4. Add to pan and fry very gently for 10 minutes, turning frequently.
5. Meanwhile, put wine, lemon juice, cream, salt, and parsley into blender. Run machine until smooth and parsley is finely chopped. Stop machine.
6. Add onions, liver, and any remaining butter or margarine to blender.
7. Quarter 2 eggs and add to blender with pepper to taste.
8. With machine at low speed, blend ingredients until they are very finely chopped and creamy.
9. Mound equal amounts on to 4 individual plates.
10. Slice remaining egg and use to garnish portions of pâté.
11. Accompany with fingers of hot toast.

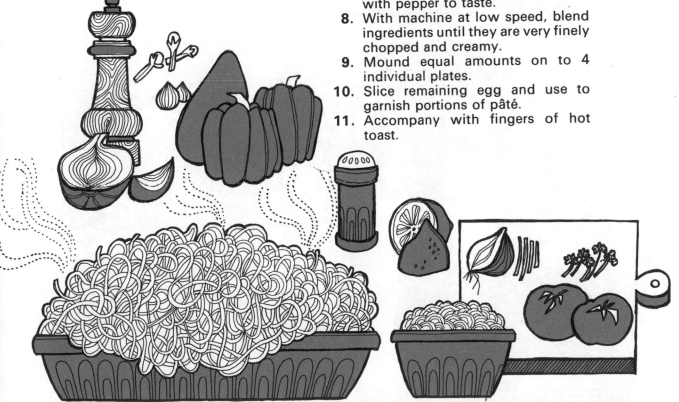

CHAPTER 2
Main Courses

This section covers dishes made from fish, shellfish, veal, beef, pork, lamb, poultry and offal, and shows how imaginative, versatile and quick one's cooking can be with the help of mixers and blenders. Traditional favourites such as Baked Meat Loaf and Beef Curry, Roast Lamb Breast, Shepherd's Pie, and Cod Steaks are all here; as are specialities from abroad including Veal Schnitzel Holstein, Wine-Braised Kidneys, Chicken Tetrazzini, Lamb Cutlets Italian, and Moules Marinière.

Fish Dishes

BAKED COD STEAKS

Serves 4

4 cod steaks
Salt and pepper
4 tablespoons milk
2 oz (50 gm) white bread, diced
½ teacup parsley
1 small onion, sliced
2 oz (50 gm) butter or margarine
4 slices tomato
A little extra butter
4 slices lemon

1. Pre-heat oven to fairly hot, 375°F or Gas No. 5 (191°C).
2. Arrange fish in buttered shallow ovenproof dish.
3. Sprinkle with salt and pepper. Pour milk into dish.
4. Put bread dice, a few at a time, into blender. Run machine until bread is reduced to fine crumbs. Tip out.
5. Put parsley and onion into blender. Run machine until finely chopped.
6. Add to crumbs and mix well.
7. Melt butter in small saucepan. Stir in crumb mixture and fry just long enough to brown slightly.
8. Sprinkle over cod steaks.
9. Season with more salt and pepper, then top with tomato slices.
10. Dot tomatoes with a little butter.
11. Cook, uncovered, in centre of oven for 20 minutes.
12. Serve garnished with lemon slices.

MARINADED SALMON STEAKS

Serves 4

4 salmon steaks
3 tablespoons salad oil
2 tablespoons lemon juice
2 tablespoons Soy sauce
2 teaspoons Worcestershire sauce
½ level teaspoon dry mustard
½ level teaspoon powdered ginger
1 small garlic clove (optional)
½ level teaspoon salt
½ level teaspoon paprika

1. Stand salmon steaks in shallow dish.
2. To make marinade, put all remaining ingredients, except parsley, into blender. Run machine until smooth. Pour over salmon steaks.
3. Leave to stand at room temperature for 1 hour, turning salmon steaks over after 30 minutes.
4. Transfer to grill pan.
5. Stand pan 3 inches (7.5 cm) below heat and grill 5 minutes.
6. Turn over, brush with marinade, and grill a further 5 to 6 minutes.
7. Garnish with parsley and serve straight away.

PIQUANT BAKED HADDOCK

Serves 4

4 pieces of haddock fillet
Salt and pepper
1 large onion, sliced
1 medium green pepper, de-seeded and diced
2 oz (50 gm) butter or margarine
2 oz (50 gm) streaky bacon, diced
4 medium tomatoes, skinned and chopped
4 tablespoons dry white wine or dry cider

1. Pre-heat oven to fairly hot, 375°F or Gas No. 5 (191°C).
2. Arrange fillets in shallow heatproof dish. Sprinkle with salt and pepper.
3. Put onion and green pepper into blender. Run machine until fairly finely chopped.
4. Melt butter or margarine in saucepan. Add onion, green pepper and bacon. Fry gently until pale gold.
5. Add tomatoes to pan. Fry a further 3 minutes, turning all the time.
6. Spoon equal amounts of fried mixture over fish fillets.
7. Pour wine or cider into dish, then cook, uncovered, in centre of oven for 30 minutes.
8. Serve straight away.

FOIL BAKED STUFFED HERRINGS

Serves 4

4 oz (100 gm) white bread, cubed
1 small onion, sliced
½ medium cooking apple, peeled, cored and sliced
3 medium celery stalks, each broken into 4 pieces
½ oz (12 gm) butter or margarine, melted
1 standard egg
2 tablespoons milk
½ level teaspoon salt
½ level teaspoon dry mustard
4 large herrings, cleaned and with backbones removed
1 extra oz (25 gm) melted butter or margarine
4 lemon slices and watercress for garnishing

1. Pre-heat oven to fairly hot, 375°F or Gas No. 5 (191°C).
2. Put bread cubes, a few at a time, into blender. Run machine until bread is reduced to fine crumbs. Tip into bowl.
3. Put onion, apple, celery, butter or margarine, egg, milk, salt, and mustard into blender. Run machine until ingredients are finely chopped.
4. Add to crumb mixture and mix thoroughly.
5. Spread equal amounts over herrings, then fold each fish in half lengthwise.
6. Stand each on a square of foil and dot with pieces of butter.
7. Sprinkle with salt, then seal foil loosely round each herring.
8. Stand on baking tray and cook in centre of oven for 30 minutes.
9. Unwrap and garnish each with lemon and watercress.

SEA FOOD CASSEROLE

Serves 4 to 5

4 oz (100 gm) Cheddar cheese, cubed
1½ lb (approximately ¾ kilo) cod or haddock fillet
1 small onion, sliced
1 level teaspoon salt
¾ pint (375 ml) milk
2 oz (50 gm) butter or margarine
2 oz (50 gm) flour
½ level teaspoon dry mustard
¼ teacup parsley
2 oz (50 gm) peeled prawns
Seasoning to taste
2 level tablespoons toasted breadcrumbs
A little extra butter or margarine

1. Pre-heat oven to fairly hot, 400°F or Gas No. 6 (204°C).
2. Put a quarter of the cheese cubes into blender. Run machine until finely chopped. Tip out on to a plate and leave on one side.
3. Put fish into shallow pan. Add onion and salt, and half-fill with water.
4. Slowly bring to boil, then poach 7 to 10 minutes or until fish flakes easily with a fork.
5. Drain fish and reserve ¼ pint (125 ml) liquor. Flake fish with 2 forks.
6. Put milk with butter or margarine into saucepan. Stand over low heat until butter melts.
7. Pour into blender. Add rest of cheese cubes, flour, mustard, and parsley.
8. Run machine until cheese and parsley are chopped.
9. Pour into saucepan and add fish liquor. Cook, stirring, until sauce comes to boil and thickens. Simmer 2 minutes.
10. Stir in flaked fish, prawns, and seasoning to taste.
11. Transfer to 2½-pint (approximately 1¼ litre) buttered heatproof dish.
12. Sprinkle top with remaining cheese mixed with breadcrumbs, then dot with flakes of butter or margarine.
13. Re-heat and brown towards top of oven for 15 to 20 minutes.

SCALLOPS MORNAY

Serves 4

8 scallops
1 level teaspoon salt
3 oz (75 gm) Cheddar cheese, diced
¼ pint (125 ml) milk
1 oz (25 gm) butter or margarine
1 oz (25 gm) flour

½ level teaspoon dry mustard
2 tablespoons double cream
Salt and pepper to taste
1 level tablespoon toasted
   breadcrumbs
Extra butter
Parsley for garnishing

1. Wash white portions and bright yellow roes of scallops.
2. Put into saucepan. Half fill with water. Add teaspoon of salt.
3. Slowly bring to boil, cover, and poach gently for 7 minutes.
4. Drain, reserving ¼ pint (125 ml) fish liquor.
5. Pat scallops dry with paper towels. Cut each into 4 or 6 slices, depending on size. Put, with roes, into buttered heatproof dish. Keep warm.
6. Put a third of cheese dice into blender. Run machine until finely chopped. Tip out on to a plate and leave on one side.
7. Put milk with butter or margarine into saucepan. Leave over low heat until butter or margarine melts.
8. Pour into blender. Add remaining cheese, flour, and mustard. Run machine until cheese is finely chopped.
9. Return to saucepan with fish liquor. Cook, stirring continuously, until sauce comes to boil and thickens. Simmer gently for 2 minutes.
10. Stir in cream, then season to taste with salt and pepper.
11. Pour over scallops, then sprinkle with reserved cheese mixed with breadcrumbs.
12. Dot with flakes of butter, then brown under a hot grill.
13. Garnish with parsley before serving.

MOULES MARINIERE

Serves 4

3 quarts (3½ litres) mussels
1 teacup parsley
1 slice white bread, cubed
3 medium onions, sliced
1 garlic clove, peeled
2 oz (50 gm) butter or margarine
¼ pint (125 ml) dry white wine
1 small bay leaf
1 level teaspoon salt

1. Cut beards from mussels with kitchen scissors.
2. Put mussels into colander and wash under cold running water, shaking colander all the time to prevent shells from opening.
3. Scrub each mussel with a stiff brush and wash again.
4. Put parsley into blender. Run machine until finely chopped. Tip out on to a plate and leave on one side. Wash and dry blender.
5. Put bread cubes, a few at a time, into blender. Run machine until bread is reduced to fine crumbs. Tip out on to a separate plate.
6. Put onions and garlic into blender. Run machine until finely chopped.
7. Melt butter or margarine in saucepan.
8. Add onions and garlic. Cover with lid.
9. Fry gently until onions are soft but not brown. Add wine, bay leaf, and salt.
10. Simmer, covered, for 10 minutes.
11. Add mussels and increase heat. Shake pan all the time until the shells open; about 8 minutes.
12. Stir in breadcrumbs, then transfer to 4 large soup plates.
13. Sprinkle equal amounts of parsley over each.

Meat & Poultry Dishes

VEAL SCHNITZEL HOLSTEIN
Serves 4

4 slices of veal fillet, each 4 to
  6 oz (100 to 150 gm)
4 large slices bread, de-crusted
  and cubed
4 level tablespoons plain flour
1 level teaspoon salt
1 large egg
2 teaspoons milk
Deep oil for frying
4 lemon slices
4 rolled anchovy fillets
4 freshly fried eggs

1. Make nicks round edges of each fillet with kitchen scissors, then beat with a rolling pin until very thin.
2. Put bread cubes, a few at a time, into blender. Run machine until reduced to fine crumbs. Tip out and leave on one side.
3. Mix flour and salt well together. Use to coat veal cutlets.
4. Lift up each cutlet and shake off surplus, then coat with egg, fork-beaten with the milk.
5. Toss in crumbs and leave to stand 15 minutes.
6. Heat oil in large frying pan, then add cutlets, two at a time.
7. Allow to fry and float in the oil for approximately 8 minutes.
8. Lift out of pan and drain on paper towels. Keep hot.
9. Fry remaining cutlets and drain.
10. Garnish each with a lemon slice and rolled anchovy, then top with a fried egg.

BAKED MEAT LOAF
Serves 4

1 lb (approximately ½ kilo) raw
  minced beef
2 large slices white or brown
  bread, cubed
1 medium onion, sliced

1 standard egg
1 tablespoon water
1 level teaspoon prepared mustard
1 level teaspoon salt
½ level teaspoon marjoram or
  mixed herbs

1. Pre-heat oven to moderate, 350°F or Gas No. 4 (177°C).
2. Put meat into bowl.
3. Put bread cubes, a few at a time, into blender. Run machine until bread is reduced to fine crumbs.
4. Add to meat in bowl.
5. Put onion, egg, water and mustard into blender. Run machine until onion is finely chopped.
6. Add to meat with salt and marjoram or mixed herbs.
7. Mix well together, then shape into loaf on aluminium foil lined baking tray.
8. Bake in centre of oven for 1 hour.
9. Serve with gravy and accompany with freshly cooked noodles or potatoes tossed in butter, and green vegetables.

QUICK LIVER AND TOMATO CASSEROLE

1 lb (approximately ½ kilo) lamb's
  liver, sliced
Milk
2 level tablespoons cornflour
1 medium onion, sliced
1 oz (25 gm) dripping
1 lb (approximately ½ kilo) cold
  cooked potatoes
1 can condensed tomato soup
5 tablespoons water
1 teaspoon Worcestershire sauce

1. Pre-heat oven to fairly hot, 375°F or Gas No. 5 (191°C).
2. Dip liver in milk, then toss in cornflour.
3. Put onion into blender. Run machine until finely chopped.
4. Melt dripping in pan. Add onion

and fry gently until pale gold.

5. Add liver and fry on both sides until crisp.
6. Put into well-greased 1½ pint (approximately ¾ litre) casserole with onions from pan. Surround with potatoes.
7. Put soup, water, and Worcestershire sauce into blender. Blend until smooth.
8. Pour into dish over liver.
9. Cover with aluminium foil.
10. Bake towards top of oven for 30 minutes.
11. Serve with peas or green beans.

CURRY OF BEEF

Serves 4

2 large onions, sliced
2 garlic cloves, peeled (optional)
2 oz (50 gm) lard or dripping
1½ lb (approximately ¾ kilo) stewing steak, cubed
1 level tablespoon flour
1 to 2 level tablespoons curry powder
½ level teaspoon powdered cinnamon
1 level teaspoon powdered ginger
2 level tablespoons canned or tubed tomato purée
1 pint (approximately ½ litre) beef stock or water
4 medium tomatoes, skinned and coarsely chopped
1 bay leaf
4 cloves
2 tablespoons sweet pickle
1 level teaspoon salt
Juice of 1 medium lemon

1. Put onions and garlic into blender. Run machine until fairly finely chopped.
2. Heat lard or dripping in large pan.
3. Add onions and garlic, and fry gently until pale gold.
4. Add beef and fry briskly until cubes are brown and well-sealed all over.
5. Put flour, curry powder, cinnamon, ginger, purée, and stock or water into blender.
6. Run machine until smooth.
7. Pour into saucepan. Cook, stirring continuously, until mixture comes to boil and thickens.

8. Add all remaining ingredients and stir well to mix.
9. Lower heat, cover pan, and simmer gently for 2 to 2½ hours, or until meat is tender.
10. Stir occasionally and add a little extra hot water if curry seems to be thickening up too much.
11. Serve with freshly boiled rice (allowing about 2 oz or 50 gm per person) and separate side dishes of plain yogurt, chutney, and slices of cucumber.

SAVOURY RICE AND LAMB BAKE

Serves 4

1 medium parsnip
2 medium onions, sliced
1 medium leek, slit lengthwise, well-washed and sliced
8 oz (200 gm) long grain rice
Salt and pepper to taste
2 lb (approximately 1 kilo) middle neck of lamb
1 level teaspoon dried basil
1 small can (approximately 8 oz or 200 gm) tomatoes
¾ pint (375 ml) hot water

1. Pre-heat oven to moderate, 350°F or Gas No. 4 (177°C).
2. Slice parsnip thinly. Arrange over base of buttered heatproof dish, large and shallow rather than deep.
3. Put onions and leek into blender. Run machine until fairly finely chopped. Arrange on top of parsnip.
4. Sprinkle rice on top, then season with salt and pepper.
5. Cut lamb into neat portions, remove as much fat as possible and arrange on top of rice. Sprinkle with basil, and more salt and pepper.
6. Put tomatoes and water into blender. Run machine until smooth.
7. Pour over lamb in dish.
8. Cover with aluminium foil and cook in centre of oven for 1½ to 2 hours.
9. Uncover dish for last 20 minutes to brown top slightly.

CHICKEN IN CIDER SAUCE WITH NOODLES

Serves 4

1 large onion, sliced
2 medium carrots, sliced
3 medium celery stalks, each broken into 4
2 oz (50 gm) butter or margarine
1 tablespoon salad oil
2 lb (approximately 1 kilo) joints of roasting chicken
2 level tablespoons cornflour
1 medium can (approximately 1 lb or ½ kilo) tomatoes
4 tablespoons canned or tubed tomato purée
½ teacup parsley
½ pint (250 ml) dry cider
1½ level teaspoons salt
1 level teaspoon basil
1 bay leaf

TO SERVE

8 to 12 oz (200 to 300 gm) freshly cooked noodles, tossed in butter

1. Pre-heat oven to moderate, 350°F or Gas No. 4 (177°C).
2. Put onion, carrots and celery into blender.
3. Run machine until fairly finely chopped.
4. Heat butter or margarine with salad oil in large flameproof casserole.
5. Add chicken joints, and fry until crisp and golden all over. Remove to plate.
6. Add chopped vegetables to casserole. Fry slowly, with lid on pan, until pale gold.
7. Put cornflour, tomatoes, purée, and parsley into blender. Run machine until smooth.
8. Add to casserole with cider, salt, basil, and bay leaf. Stir well to mix.
9. Bring to boil, stirring continuously. Replace chicken. Cover casserole.
10. Cook in centre of oven for 1½ hours, stirring occasionally.
11. Serve with noodles and a large green salad.

DEVILLED PORK CHOPS

Serves 4

4 thick pork chops, each 6 oz (150 gm) in weight
4 level tablespoons flour
1 level teaspoon salt
1 oz (25 gm) butter or margarine
2 tablespoons salad oil
4 tablespoons water
4 level tablespoons tomato ketchup
1 level tablespoon Soy sauce
2 level tablespoons brown sugar
2 teaspoons Worcestershire sauce
½ level teaspoon dry mustard
3 tablespoons vinegar
1 large onion, sliced

1. Coat chops on both sides with flour mixed with salt.

2. Heat butter or margarine with 1 tablespoon oil in skillet or large frying pan.
3. Add chops and fry on both sides until crisp and golden.
4. Put second tablespoon of oil into blender with all remaining ingredients.
5. Run machine until onion is finely chopped.
6. Pour into skillet or pan over chops.
7. Slowly bring to boil, stirring.
8. Lower heat and cover pan. Simmer 45 minutes, or until chops are cooked through.
9. Serve with plain boiled rice (allowing 2 to 3 oz, 50 to 75 gm, per person) and a selection of green vegetables.

WINE-BRAISED KIDNEYS

Serves 4

1 large onion, sliced
1 oz (25 gm) butter or margarine
1 lb (approximately $\frac{1}{2}$ kilo) ox kidney, cubed
4 oz (100 gm) lean bacon
1 oz (25 gm) flour
$\frac{1}{4}$ pint (125 ml) water
$\frac{1}{4}$ pint (125 ml) dry red wine
$\frac{1}{4}$ teacup parsley
1 level teaspoon salt
Pepper to taste

1. Pre-heat oven to moderate, 350°F or Gas No. 4 (177°C).
2. Put onion into blender. Run machine until finely chopped.
3. Melt butter or margarine in saucepan. Add onion and fry gently until soft but not brown.
4. Add kidney and bacon, and fry a little more briskly until crisp and golden.
5. Put all remaining ingredients into blender. Run machine until smooth.
6. Pour into pan. Stir well to mix. Bring to boil, stirring continuously.
7. Transfer to buttered casserole dish and cover with lid or aluminium foil.
8. Cook in centre of oven for approximately $1\frac{1}{2}$ hours or until kidney is tender.
9. Serve with freshly boiled potatoes and a tossed salad.

TURKEY DIVAN

Serves 4

8 cream crackers
8 large turkey slices, cut from breast
1 large packet frozen broccoli, already cooked
$\frac{3}{4}$ pint (375 ml) milk
$1\frac{1}{2}$ oz (37 gm) butter
$1\frac{1}{2}$ oz (37 gm) flour
3 oz (75 gm) Cheddar cheese, diced
Salt and pepper to taste
6 rounded teaspoons grated Parmesan cheese

1. Pre-heat oven to fairly hot, 400°F or Gas No. 6 (204°C).
2. Break up crackers. Put a few at a time into blender. Run machine until reduced to coarse crumbs.
3. Sprinkle over base of buttered, shallow heatproof dish.
4. Cover with turkey slices, then arrange broccoli on top.
5. Put milk and butter into a saucepan and leave over low heat until butter melts.
6. Pour into blender. Add flour and cheese dice. Run machine until cheese is finely chopped.
7. Return to saucepan. Cook, stirring continuously, until sauce comes to boil and thickens. Simmer 2 minutes, then season to taste with salt and pepper.
8. Use to cover ingredients in dish.
9. Sprinkle with Parmesan cheese and cook near top of oven until golden and bubbly; about 15 to 20 minutes.

LAMB CUTLETS ITALIAN

Serves 4

5 tablespoons salad oil
3 slices white bread, cubed
3 heaped tablespoons Parmesan
  cheese
2 standard eggs
1 tablespoon milk
8 lamb cutlets

1. Pre-heat oven to fairly hot, 400°F
   or Gas No. 6 (204°C).
2. Pour oil into medium-sized roasting
   tin. Put into centre of oven.
3. Put bread cubes, a few at a time,
   into blender. Run machine until
   bread is reduced to fine crumbs.
4. Combine crumbs with cheese.
5. Fork-beat eggs with milk.
6. Coat cutlets with egg mixture, then
   toss in crumbs.
7. Leave 5 minutes. Coat once more
   with egg and crumb mixture.
8. Remove tin from oven and put in
   cutlets.
9. Baste with hot oil and cook towards
   top of oven for 20 minutes.
10. Drain thoroughly on paper towels,
    then serve with Tomato Sauce
    (page 37), fried potatoes and a
    green salad.

GLAZED STUFFED CHICKEN

Serves 4 to 6

1 roasting chicken, weighing
  about 4 lb (2 kilo)
Stuffing to taste (see Stuffings,
  pages 30–32)

GLAZE

1 medium orange, peeled
1 tablespoon olive oil
1 teaspoon Worcestershire sauce
1 tablespoon golden syrup

1. Pre-heat oven to very hot, 450°F or
   Gas No. 8 (232°C).
2. Wash chicken under cold running
   water and leave to drain.
3. Pack body cavity of chicken with
   stuffing and stand in roasting tin.
4. Put into centre of oven and at once
   reduce oven temperature to moderate, 350°F or Gas No. 4 (177°C).
5. Roast for 1¼ hours.

6. To make glaze, slice orange and put
   into blender with oil, Worcestershire sauce, and syrup. Run machine
   until smooth. Tip into bowl.
7. Remove chicken from oven and
   brush heavily with glaze. Roast a
   further ¾ hour, brushing with glaze
   two or three times more.

CHICKEN TETRAZZINI

Serves 4

2 oz (50 gm) Cheddar cheese,
  cubed
6 oz (150 gm) elbow macaroni
6 oz (150 gm) mushrooms, sliced
2 oz (50 gm) butter
1½ oz (37 gm) flour
½ pint (250 ml) chicken stock
¼ pint (125 ml) cold milk
4 tablespoons double cream
3 tablespoons dry white wine
Salt and pepper to taste
12 oz (300 gm) cold cooked
  chicken, diced

1. Pre-heat oven to fairly hot, 375°F
   or Gas No. 5 (191°C).
2. Put cheese cubes, a few at a time,
   into blender. Run machine until
   finely chopped. Tip out on to a
   plate and leave on one side.
3. Cook macaroni as directed on the
   packet. Drain.
4. Fry mushrooms in butter for 5
   minutes. Lift out of pan (leaving
   butter behind) and stir thoroughly
   into macaroni.
5. Put flour, stock and milk into
   blender. Run machine until smooth.
6. Pour into pan in which mushrooms
   were fried. Cook, stirring continuously, until sauce comes to boil and
   thickens. Simmer 2 minutes.
7. Remove from heat, and stir in cream
   and wine. Season to taste with
   salt and pepper.
8. Combine half the sauce with
   macaroni and mushrooms, and
   arrange over base of shallow, heatproof dish.
9. Combine rest of sauce with diced
   chicken and spoon over macaroni.
10. Sprinkle with cheese, then reheat
    and brown towards top of oven for
    approximately 20 minutes.
11. Serve with a green salad.

22

ROAST LAMB BREAST

2 lamb breasts, boned and
   trimmed of surplus fat
1 garlic clove
2 medium celery stalks, each
   broken into 4
1 oz (25 gm) butter or margarine
6 oz (150 gm) white bread, diced
1 level teaspoon dried rosemary
1 teaspoon Worcestershire sauce
Salt and pepper to taste
1 standard egg, fork-beaten
Milk

1. Pre-heat oven to fairly hot, 400°F
   or Gas No. 6 (204°C).
2. Spread out lamb breasts and rub
   with cut clove of garlic.
3. Put celery stalks into blender. Run
   machine until coarsely chopped.
4. Fry slowly in butter or margarine
   until pale golden.
5. Put bread dice, a few at a time, into
   blender. Run machine until reduced
   to fine crumbs.
6. Combine with celery and any remaining butter or margarine from
   pan.
7. Add rosemary and Worcestershire
   sauce, then season to taste with
   salt and pepper.
8. Bind with egg, adding milk only if
   necessary.

9. Spread equal amounts over lamb
   breasts, roll each up, and hold in
   place by tying with string.
10. Transfer to roasting tin, sprinkle
    with salt and pepper, and roast in
    centre of oven for 1 hour.
11. Untie, cut into slices, and serve with
    gravy, new potatoes and green
    vegetables to taste.

STUFFED GAMMON ROLL HOT POT

Serves 4

3 oz (75 gm) fresh white bread,
   cubed
2 canned pineapple rings
$\frac{1}{4}$ teacup parsley
$\frac{1}{2}$ small onion, sliced
1 oz (25 gm) butter, melted
1 standard egg
Cold milk
Salt and pepper to taste
4 large gammon rashers, no more
   than $\frac{1}{4}$ inch thick
$\frac{1}{4}$ pint (125 ml) chicken stock
4 tablespoons syrup from can of
   pineapple

1. Pre-heat oven to fairly hot, 375°F
   or Gas No. 5 (191°C).
2. Put bread cubes, a few at a time,
   into blender. Run machine until
   bread is reduced to fine crumbs.
3. Break up pineapple rings into large
   pieces. Add to blender with parsley,
   onion, butter, and egg.
4. Blend until pineapple and onion
   are finely chopped.
5. Add to crumb mixture. Stir thoroughly with a fork, adding a little
   cold milk if necessary to bind
   ingredients. Season with salt and
   pepper.
6. Spread equal amounts over gammon rashers. Roll up and secure
   with cocktail sticks.
7. Put into casserole dish and add
   stock mixed with pineapple syrup.
8. Cover dish with lid or aluminium
   foil and bake in centre of oven for
   30 minutes.

Note

To ensure gammon is not over salty, soak
for 2 to 4 hours in two changes of cold
water before using.

23

SHEPHERD'S PIE LYONNAISE

2 large onions, sliced
1½ oz (37 gm) butter or margarine
8 to 12 oz (200 to 300 gm) cold
   cooked minced lamb or beef
1 oz (25 gm) flour
½ pint (250 ml) water
1 level teaspoon beef extract
1 teaspoon Worcestershire sauce
Salt and pepper to taste
1 lb (approximately ½ kilo) freshly
   boiled potatoes
1 oz (25 gm) butter
4 tablespoons hot milk

1. Pre-heat oven to fairly hot, 400°F or Gas No. 6 (204°C).
2. Put onions into blender. Run machine until finely chopped.
3. Melt butter or margarine in saucepan. Add onions and fry gently until pale golden. Remove half the onions and keep on one side.
4. Add minced meat to pan and fry over medium heat for 5 minutes.
5. Meanwhile, put flour, water, beef extract and Worcestershire sauce into blender. Run machine until smooth.
6. Pour into pan over meat. Cook, stirring continuously, until mixture comes to boil and thickens. Season to taste with salt and pepper.
7. Lower heat, cover pan, and simmer 20 minutes.
8. Put potatoes into mixer bowl and break up with fork.
9. Add butter and hot milk. With mixer at low speed, cream with beaters until light and fluffy. Stir in rest of fried onions. Adjust seasoning to taste.
10. Put meat into well-buttered heatproof dish.
11. Pile potatoes on top, swirling them with a fork.
12. Re-heat towards top of oven for 25 to 30 minutes, or until potatoes are lightly browned.

APPLE GLAZED LEG OF LAMB ROAST

1 large onion, sliced
1 large cooking apple, peeled,
   cored and thinly sliced
2 oz (50 gm) butter or margarine
6 oz (150 gm) white bread, diced
2 tomatoes, skinned and chopped
2 oz (50 gm) sultanas or seedless
   raisins
½ level teaspoon mixed herbs
Salt and pepper to taste
1 standard egg, fork-beaten
Milk
1 leg of lamb, weighing about 4 lb
   (2 kilo), boned

GLAZE

2 oz (50 gm) soft brown sugar
5 tablespoons apple juice
1 tablespoon Worcestershire
   sauce

1. Pre-heat oven to fairly hot, 375°F or Gas No. 5 (191°C).
2. Put onion and apple into blender. Run machine until coarsely chopped.
3. Fry slowly in the butter or margarine until pale golden.
4. Put bread cubes, a few at a time, into blender. Run machine until reduced to fine crumbs.
5. Combine with fried onion and apple, and any remaining butter or margarine from pan.
6. Stir in tomatoes, sultanas or raisins, and mixed herbs.
7. Season to taste with salt and pepper, then bind with egg and a little milk if necessary.
8. Pack into lamb and secure both ends by tying with string.
9. Transfer joint to roasting tin and coat with glaze made by dissolving the brown sugar in the apple juice and Worcestershire sauce, and then boiling for 2 minutes.
10. Roast 2 hours, basting frequently.

Vegetarian Dishes

PIQUANT MUSHROOM COCKTAIL

Serves 4

Shredded lettuce
¼ pint (125 ml) thick Mayonnaise (page 36)
3 teaspoons lemon juice
½ teacup parsley
2 tablespoons stuffed olives
½ teaspoon yeast extract
Salt and pepper to taste
8 oz (200 gm) raw button mushrooms, peeled, washed and thinly sliced
4 extra stuffed olives, sliced for garnishing

1. One-third fill 4 large wine glasses with shredded lettuce.
2. Put mayonnaise into blender. Add lemon juice, parsley, olives, and yeast extract.
3. Run machine just long enough to chop parsley and olives into fairly small pieces.
4. Tip into bowl. Season to taste with salt and pepper, and stir in mushrooms.
5. Spoon equal amounts into glasses and garnish each with sliced olives.
6. Chill lightly before serving.

EGG AND CASHEW COCKTAIL

Serves 4

Shredded lettuce
4 hard-boiled eggs, quartered
4 dessertspoons natural yogurt
4 dessertspoons thick Mayonnaise (page 36)
1 level teaspoon prepared mustard
½ teaspoon Worcestershire sauce
½ teaspoon yeast extract
2 teaspoons canned or tubed tomato purée
Salt and pepper to taste
4 dessertspoons cashew nuts, toasted
Curry powder

1. One-third fill 4 large wine glasses with shredded lettuce.
2. Put eggs into blender. Add yogurt, mayonnaise, mustard, Worcestershire sauce, yeast extract, and tomato purée.
3. Run machine just long enough to chop eggs into fairly small pieces.
4. Tip into bowl. Season to taste with salt and pepper, and stir in the cashews.
5. Spoon equal amounts into glasses and sprinkle top of each lightly with curry powder.
6. Chill lightly before serving.

PUFFY RAREBIT TOASTS

Serves 4

4 large slices white bread
6 oz (150 gm) Cheddar cheese, cubed
1½ oz (37 gm) softened butter or margarine
½ teaspoon yeast extract
3 dessertspoons milk
1 large egg, separated
½ level teaspoon prepared mustard
½ teaspoon Worcestershire sauce
Pinch of Cayenne pepper
Salt to taste

1. Toast bread on one side only.
2. Put cheese cubes into blender, about one-third at a time. Blend on low speed until all are finely chopped.
3. Combine with butter or margarine, yeast extract, milk, egg yolk, mustard, Worcestershire sauce, Cayenne pepper, and salt to taste.
4. Put egg white into clean, dry mixer bowl.
5. Beat with beaters until stiff.
6. With metal spoon, fold into cheese mixture.
7. Spread on untoasted sides of bread.
8. Brown under a hot grill and serve straight away.

TOMATO PIZZA

Serves 4

8 oz (200 gm) wholemeal self-raising flour
1 level teaspoon salt
1 oz (25 gm) butter or margarine
$\frac{1}{4}$ pint (125 ml) cold milk

FILLING

1 medium onion
1 tablespoon salad oil
4 tablespoons canned or tubed tomato purée
1 level teaspoon yeast extract
2 level teaspoons soft brown sugar
$\frac{1}{4}$ level teaspoon salt
5 oz (125 gm) Cheddar cheese, cubed
4 large tomatoes, skinned

1. Pre-heat oven to hot, 425°F or Gas No. 7 (218°C).
2. Sift flour and salt into bowl.
3. Cut butter or margarine into small pieces and add to flour.
4. With mixer at low speed, run beaters through ingredients until they resemble fine breadcrumbs.
5. Add milk all at once and mix to a soft dough with a knife.
6. Turn out on to floured surface and knead lightly until smooth.
7. Roll into an 8 inch (20 cm) round and transfer to well-greased baking tray.
8. Slice onion and put into blender.

9. Heat oil in saucepan. Add onion and fry until golden.
10. Stir in all remaining ingredients except cheese and tomatoes.
11. Cook gently for 2 minutes, then spread over Pizza base to within $\frac{1}{2}$ inch (1.2 cm) of edges.
12. Put cheese cubes, a few at a time, into blender. Blend at low speed until finely chopped.
13. Pile cheese over filling.
14. Slice tomatoes and arrange on top of cheese.
15. Bake just above centre of oven for 25 to 30 minutes.
16. Cut into wedges and serve straight away.

CHEESE TARTS

Makes 12

4 oz (100 gm) Short Crust Pastry (page 63)
8 oz (200 gm) curd cheese
1 level dessertspoon cornflour
1 dessertspoon milk
$\frac{1}{4}$ level teaspoon prepared mustard
1 large egg, separated
Salt and pepper to taste

1. Pre-heat oven to very hot, 450°F or Gas No. 8 (232°C).
2. Roll out pastry thinly.
3. Cut into 12 rounds with 3 inch (7.5 cm) biscuit cutter. Use to line 12 bun tins.
4. Put cheese, cornflour, milk, mustard, and egg yolk into basin.
5. Mix with a fork until well-blended.
6. Put egg white into clean, dry mixer bowl.
7. With mixer at high speed, beat with beaters until stiff.
8. Using a metal spoon, fold into cheese mixture.
9. Season to taste with salt and pepper.
10. Spoon equal amounts into pastry-lined tins.
11. Put into centre of oven and at once reduce temperature to moderate, 350°F or Gas No. 4 (177°C).
12. Bake 20 minutes, then carefully remove from tins.
13. Cool on a wire rack.
14. Eat warm or cold.

COTTAGE CHEESE AND PEACH MOUSSE SALAD

Serves 6

6 large lettuce leaves
6 peach halves, well-drained
8 oz (200 gm) cottage cheese
2 heaped tablespoons soured
  cream
1 level teaspoon continental
  mustard
½ teaspoon Worcestershire sauce
¼ level teaspoon powdered ginger
Salt to taste
1 egg white
Paprika
Watercress for garnishing

1. Stand lettuce on 6 individual plates.
2. Top each with a peach half, cut side uppermost.
3. Put cottage cheese into bowl. Using a fork, stir in soured cream, mustard, Worcestershire sauce, ginger, and salt to taste.
4. Put egg white into clean, dry mixer bowl.
5. With mixer at high speed, beat with beaters until stiff. Fold into cheese mixture with metal spoon.
6. Pile equal amounts over peaches, then sprinkle lightly with paprika.
7. Garnish with watercress and serve straight away.

CRISPY CHEESE RISSOLES

Serves 4

8 oz (200 gm) brown bread, diced
6 oz (150 gm) Cheddar cheese,
  cubed
½ level teaspoon dry mustard
1 level teaspoon onion, finely
  grated
½ level teaspoon paprika
¼ level teaspoon chilli powder
¼ pint (125 ml) hot milk
1 standard egg, beaten
Salt and pepper to taste

1. Put bread dice, a few at a time, into blender. Run machine until bread is reduced to fine crumbs.
2. Put cheese cubes, a few at a time, into blender and blend on low speed until very finely chopped.
3. Put crumbs and cheese into bowl.

4. Add all remaining ingredients and mix thoroughly with a fork.
5. Leave until cold, then shape into 8 cakes.
6. Fry in hot oil until golden brown on both sides.
7. Drain on paper towels.
8. Serve hot with a green vegetable and creamy mashed potatoes.

CURRIED RICE

Serves 4

1 large onion
2 canned red pimiento caps
1 tablespoon salad oil
4 oz (100 gm) long grain rice
1 to 1½ level tablespoons curry
  powder
½ pint (250 ml) water
1 bay leaf
½ to 1 level teaspoon salt
1 tablespoon chutney

1. Slice onion and pimiento caps.
2. Put into blender and run machine until both are roughly chopped.
3. Add onion and pimiento to hot oil in saucepan. Cover and fry gently for 10 minutes, shaking pan often.
4. Uncover and continue to fry until onions are pale golden.
5. Add rice and fry a further minute, turning all the time.
6. Stir in all remaining ingredients.
7. Bring to boil, lower heat and stir once with a fork.
8. Cover and simmer for 15 to 20 minutes, or until rice grains are plump and tender, and have absorbed all the liquid.

HOME MADE PEANUT BUTTER

8 oz (200 gm) salted peanuts
3 tablespoons groundnut oil
1 level teaspoon yeast extract

1. Put nuts into blender. Run machine until finely chopped.
2. Stop machine, and add oil and yeast extract.
3. Run machine for 1 minute. Stop machine and stir. Continue to blend until mixture is smooth and creamy; about 1 further minute.
4. Store in a screw-topped jar.

JACKET POTATO CREAMS

Serves 4

4 medium potatoes
4 tablespoons milk
2 oz (50 gm) butter or margarine
4 oz (100 gm) Cheddar cheese, diced
1 to 1½ level teaspoons salt
1 level teaspoon dry mustard
Shake of Cayenne pepper

TOPPING

¼ pint (125 ml) soured cream
Paprika

1. Pre-heat oven to fairly hot, 375°F or Gas No. 5 (191°C).
2. Wash and dry potatoes. Prick skins all over with fork.
3. Put on to lightly oiled baking tray.
4. Cook in centre of oven for 1½ to 2 hours, or until tender.
5. Remove from oven. Slit in half lengthwise and spoon insides into mixer bowl. Leave shells on baking tray.
6. Put milk and butter or margarine into saucepan. Heat gently until butter or margarine is melted.
7. Put into blender with diced cheese, salt, mustard, and Cayenne pepper.
8. Run machine until cheese is very finely chopped.
9. Add to potatoes.
10. With mixer at low speed, beat with beaters until potatoes are light and creamy.
11. Return to potato shells and top with soured cream.
12. Sprinkle with paprika and return to oven for a further 15 minutes to heat through.

STUFFED PEPPERS

Serves 4

4 oz (100 gm) Cheddar cheese, diced
1 medium onion, sliced
1 dessertspoon salad oil
4 oz (100 gm) long grain rice
½ pint (250 ml) water
1 level teaspoon yeast extract
Salt and pepper to taste
4 medium green peppers
Hot water

1. Put cheese dice, a few at a time, into blender. Blend on low speed until finely chopped. Tip out and leave on one side. Rinse and dry blender.
2. Put onion into blender and run machine until finely chopped.
3. Heat oil in saucepan. Add onion and fry until pale golden.
4. Add rice and fry a further minute, turning all the time.
5. Pour in water, then add yeast extract, and salt and pepper.
6. Bring to boil, stir once, and cover.
7. Lower heat and simmer slowly for 20 minutes, or until rice grains are plump and tender, and have absorbed all the moisture.
8. Meanwhile, cut tops off peppers, and remove inside fibres and seeds.
9. Wash thoroughly, and stand close together and upright in saucepan.
10. Half-fill pan with hot water, add 1 or 2 teaspoons salt, and slowly bring to boil. Simmer 8 minutes.
11. Drain thoroughly.
12. Stir cheese into rice, adjust seasoning to taste, and spoon equal amounts into peppers.
13. Serve straight away.

FEATHER-LIGHT LANCASHIRE BAKE

Serves 4

3 large slices white bread, diced
½ pint (250 ml) milk
1 level teaspoon yeast extract
4 oz (100 gm) Lancashire cheese, finely crumbled
½ level teaspoon dry mustard
½ teaspoon Worcestershire sauce
½ level teaspoon paprika
2 standard eggs, separated
Salt and pepper to taste

1. Pre-heat oven to fairly hot, 375°F or Gas No. 5 (191°C).
2. Put bread dice, a few at a time, into blender. Run machine until bread is reduced to fine crumbs. Put into bowl.
3. Heat milk to lukewarm with yeast extract.
4. Add crumbs. Using a fork, whisk over low heat until mixture becomes thick and smooth.

5. Beat in cheese, mustard, Worcestershire sauce, paprika, and egg yolks.
6. Remove from heat, and season to taste with salt and pepper.
7. Put egg whites into clean, dry mixer bowl.
8. With mixer at high speed, beat with beaters until whites are stiff and peaky.
9. Using a metal spoon, fold into cheese and crumb mixture.
10. Transfer to buttered deep 2½ pint (1¼ litre) ovenproof dish and bake in centre of oven for 35 to 40 minutes, or until well-puffed and golden.
11. Serve straight away.

NUTBURGERS

Serves 4

2 oz (50 gm) Brazil nuts
2 oz (50 gm) cashew nuts
3 oz (75 gm) brown bread, diced
1 medium onion, sliced
1 teaspoon yeast extract
1 large egg
1 tablespoon hot water
½ to 1 level teaspoon salt
Oil or margarine for frying

1. Coarsely chop Brazil nuts.
2. Combine with cashews.
3. Put nuts, a few at a time, into blender. Run machine until finely chopped, but do not allow machine to over-run or nuts will become paste-like and oily. Tip into bowl.
4. Put bread dice, a few at a time, into blender. Run machine until bread is reduced to fine crumbs. Add to nuts.
5. Put all remaining ingredients, except oil and margarine, into blender. Run machine until onion is finely chopped.
6. Add to nut and breadcrumb mixture, and stir until well-combined. Leave to stand for 10 minutes.
7. Shape into 8 cakes.
8. Fry in hot oil or margarine until crisp and golden on both sides.
9. Drain on paper towels.
10. Serve hot or cold.

NUT LOAF

Serves 4

4 oz (100 gm) hazelnuts
2 oz (50 gm) cashew nuts
2 oz (50 gm) shelled walnut halves
6 oz (150 gm) brown bread, diced
1 medium onion, sliced
2 level teaspoons salt
½ teacup parsley
2 teaspoons yeast extract
5 tablespoons hot milk
Pepper to taste

1. Pre-heat oven to moderate, 350°F or Gas No. 4 (177°C).
2. Brush baking tray with melted butter or margarine.
3. Put nuts, a few at a time, into blender. Run machine until finely chopped, but do not allow machine to over-run or nuts will become paste-like and oily. Tip into bowl.
4. Put bread dice, a few at a time, into blender. Run machine until bread is reduced to fine crumbs. Add to nuts.
5. Put all remaining ingredients into blender. Run machine until onion is finely chopped.
6. Add to nut and crumb mixture and combine thoroughly with a fork.
7. Shape into a 2 inch (5 cm) high loaf and stand on prepared tray.
8. Bake in centre of oven for 45 minutes.
9. Serve hot or cold.

29

MACARONI AU GRATIN

Serves 4

½ oz (12 gm) brown bread, diced
4 oz (100 gm) elbow macaroni
1 oz (25 gm) butter or margarine
¾ pint (375 ml) milk
1 oz (25 gm) flour
3 oz (75 gm) Cheddar cheese, diced
1 level teaspoon prepared mustard
Pinch of Cayenne pepper
½ teaspoon Worcestershire sauce
Salt and pepper to taste
½ oz (12 gm) extra butter or margarine

1. Pre-heat oven to hot, 425°F or Gas No. 7 (218°C).
2. Put bread dice, a few at a time, into blender. Run machine until bread is reduced to fine crumbs. Tip on to a plate and leave on one side.
3. Cook macaroni in boiling salted water as directed on the packet.
4. Put 1 oz (25 gm) butter or margarine and milk into a saucepan.
5. Heat until butter or margarine melts.
6. Pour into blender. Add all remaining ingredients except extra butter.
7. Run machine until cheese is finely chopped.
8. Return to saucepan. Cook, stirring continuously, until sauce comes to boil and thickens.
9. Simmer 2 minutes on low heat.
10. Drain macaroni very thoroughly. Add to cheese sauce and mix well.
11. Transfer to buttered 2 pint (approximately 1¼ litre) heatproof dish.
12. Sprinkle brown crumbs over the top, then dot with flakes of butter or margarine.
13. Bake near the top of oven for 15 minutes.

Stuffings

PARSLEY, LEMON, AND THYME STUFFING

4 oz (100 gm) white bread, cubed
1 oz (25 gm) finely shredded suet
½ teacup parsley
2 inch (5 cm) strip of lemon rind
1 standard egg
½ level teaspoon thyme
Salt and pepper to taste
Milk

1. Put bread cubes, a few at a time, into blender. Blend until bread is reduced to fine crumbs. Put into bowl. Add suet.
2. Put parsley, lemon rind, and egg into blender. Blend until parsley and rind are finely chopped.
3. Add to crumb mixture with thyme, and salt and pepper to taste.
4. Stir well to combine, then bind with a little milk if necessary.
5. Use for poultry, fish and veal.

PILAF STUFFING

1 medium onion, sliced
1 oz (25 gm) bacon dripping or margarine
4 oz (100 gm) long grain rice
½ pint (250 ml) stock or water
2 oz (50 gm) seedless raisins
2 oz (50 gm) flaked almonds
Salt and pepper to taste

1. Put onion into blender. Run machine until onion is finely chopped.
2. Melt dripping or margarine in pan. Add onion and fry gently until pale gold.
3. Add rice and fry a further minute.
4. Pour in stock or water and bring to boil.
5. Add raisins, almonds, and salt and pepper to taste. Stir once or twice with a fork.
6. Lower heat, cover, and cook about

20 minutes, or until rice grains are tender and plump, and have absorbed all the liquid.
7. Leave until cold before using.
8. Use to stuff poultry.

SAGE AND ONION STUFFING

8 oz (200 gm) onions, quartered
4 oz (100 gm) white bread, cubed
1 level teaspoon dried sage
1 oz (25 gm) finely shredded suet
Salt and pepper to taste
Milk

1. Cook onions in boiling salted water until tender.
2. Put bread cubes, a few at a time, into blender. Blend until bread is reduced to fine crumbs.
3. Put into bowl. Add sage and suet.
4. Drain onions and put into blender. Run machine until finely chopped.
5. Add to crumb mixture with salt and pepper to taste. Bind with milk.
6. Use to stuff pork, duck and goose.

LAMB, GARLIC, AND ROSEMARY STUFFING

12 oz (300 gm) raw minced lamb (cut from leg)
1 garlic clove, peeled
$\frac{1}{2}$ teacup parsley
1 standard egg
1 level teaspoon dried rosemary
Salt and pepper to taste

1. Put lamb into bowl.
2. Put garlic, parsley and egg into blender.
3. Run machine until garlic and parsley are finely chopped.
4. Add to lamb with rosemary, and salt and pepper to taste. Mix well with fork.
5. Draw stuffing together with fingertips.
6. Use to stuff chicken, turkey, and veal.

VEAL AND ORANGE STUFFING

12 oz (300 gm) raw pie veal, minced
3 inch (7.5 cm) strip of orange rind

$\frac{1}{2}$ small onion, sliced
1 standard egg
1 level teaspoon dried thyme
Salt and pepper to taste

1. Follow recipe for Lamb, Garlic, and Rosemary Stuffing.
2. Use to stuff pork, lamb, beef, poultry, duck, and goose.

SPICY BEEF STUFFING

12 oz (300 gm) raw beef, minced
1 medium onion, sliced
1 teaspoon Worcestershire sauce
1 standard egg
$\frac{1}{4}$ level teaspoon nutmeg
Salt and pepper to taste

1. Follow recipe for Lamb, Garlic, and Rosemary Stuffing.
2. Use to stuff beef, lamb, veal, and poultry.

BRAZIL AND PEANUT STUFFING

8 oz (200 gm) Brazil nuts
4 oz (100 gm) unsalted peanuts
2 level teaspoons dry mustard
$\frac{1}{2}$ level teaspoon paprika
Salt and pepper to taste
1 standard egg, fork-beaten

1. Coarsely chop Brazil nuts. Combine with peanuts.
2. Put, a few at a time, into blender. Run machine until nuts are finely chopped, but do not allow machine to over-run or nuts will become paste-like and oily. Tip into bowl.
3. Add mustard, paprika, and salt and pepper to taste.
4. Stir in egg, then draw stuffing together with fingertips.
5. Use for poultry, beef, fish, veal and duck.

SAUSAGEMEAT STUFFING

8 oz (200 gm) pork sausagemeat
  or skinned pork sausages
$\frac{1}{4}$ level teaspoon dry mustard
1 oz (25 gm) white bread, diced
1 medium onion, sliced
$\frac{1}{4}$ teacup parsley
Salt and pepper to taste

1. Put sausagemeat into bowl. Add mustard.
2. Put bread dice, a few at a time, into blender. Run machine until bread is reduced to fine crumbs. Add to sausagemeat.
3. Put onion into blender with parsley.
4. Run machine until both are finely chopped.
5. Add to sausagemeat with salt and pepper to taste. Mix well with fork.
6. Use to stuff poultry, veal, and beef.

CHESTNUT STUFFING

1 lb (approximately $\frac{1}{2}$ kilo)
  chestnuts
4 oz (100 gm) white bread, diced
1 medium onion, sliced
1 standard egg
2 oz (50 gm) melted butter or
  margarine
Salt and pepper to taste

1. Make a slit in each chestnut and cook in boiling salted water for 45 minutes to 1 hour, or until tender.
2. Drain, peel and break chestnuts into pieces.
3. Put bread dice, a few at a time, into blender. Run machine until bread is reduced to fine crumbs. Tip into bowl.
4. Put chestnuts into blender with onion, egg, and melted butter or margarine. Blend until smooth.
5. Add to crumb mixture with salt and pepper to taste. Mix thoroughly with a fork and draw stuffing together with fingertips.
6. Use to stuff poultry.

APPLE AND RAISIN STUFFING

4 oz (100 gm) white bread, diced
$\frac{1}{2}$ medium onion, sliced
1 lb (approximately $\frac{1}{2}$ kilo)
  cooking apples
2 to 3 oz (50 to 75 gm) seedless
  raisins
1 level teaspoon salt
Freshly milled black pepper to
taste
2 oz (50 gm) melted butter or
  margarine
Milk

1. Put bread dice, a few at a time, into blender. Run machine until bread is reduced to fine crumbs. Put into bowl.
2. Put onion into blender.
3. Run machine until finely chopped. Add to crumbs.
4. Peel, core, and coarsely chop apples.
5. Add to crumb mixture with raisins, and salt and pepper to taste.
6. Using a fork, stir in butter or margarine, then bind with a little milk.
7. Use to stuff duck, goose, and pork.

Sauces

BASIC WHITE SAUCE

$\frac{1}{2}$ pint (250 ml) cold milk
1 oz (25 gm) butter or margarine
1 oz (25 gm) flour
Salt and pepper to taste

1. Put milk into saucepan with butter or margarine.
2. Heat gently until butter or margarine melts.
3. Pour into blender. Add flour and seasonings. Run machine until

ingredients are smoothly blended.
4. Return to saucepan.
5. Cook, stirring continuously, until sauce comes to boil and thickens.
6. Simmer 2 minutes over low heat.

PARSLEY SAUCE

1. Follow recipe for Basic White Sauce, adding 2 heaped tablespoons of parsley sprigs to mixture in blender.

ANCHOVY SAUCE

Suitable for all fish dishes

½ pint (250 ml) cold milk
1 oz (25 gm) butter or margarine
1 oz (25 gm) flour
2 teaspoons anchovy essence
2 teaspoons lemon juice
Salt and pepper to taste

1. Put milk into saucepan with butter or margarine.
2. Heat gently until butter or margarine melts.
3. Pour into blender.
4. Add all remaining ingredients except salt. Run machine until ingredients are well-blended.
5. Return to saucepan.
6. Cook, stirring continuously, until sauce comes to the boil and thickens. Season to taste with salt.
7. Simmer 2 minutes over low heat.

CHEESE SAUCE

½ pint (250 ml) cold milk
1 oz (25 gm) butter or margarine
3 oz (75 gm) Cheddar cheese, cubed
1 oz (25 gm) flour
½ to 1 level teaspoon made mustard
Pinch of Cayenne pepper
Salt to taste

1. Put milk into saucepan with butter or margarine.
2. Heat gently until butter or margarine melts.
3. Pour into blender.
4. Add cheese cubes and all remaining ingredients. Run machine until cheese is fairly finely chopped.

5. Return to saucepan.
6. Cook, stirring continuously, until sauce comes to boil and thickens.
7. Simmer 2 minutes over low heat.

EGG SAUCE

Pleasant with white fish and poultry dishes

½ pint (250 ml) cold milk
1 oz (25 gm) butter or margarine
1 oz (25 gm) flour
2 standard eggs, hard-boiled and quartered
Salt and pepper to taste

1. Follow recipe for Cheese Sauce up to step 4.
2. Put eggs in blender with rest of ingredients. Run machine until eggs are coarsely chopped.
3. Complete as Cheese Sauce.

BÉCHAMEL SAUCE

½ pint (250 ml) milk
1 small onion, peeled and halved
1 small carrot, peeled and coarsely sliced
1 small celery stalk, broken into 4 pieces
1 blade mace
1 large parsley sprig
3 cloves
½ small bay leaf
3 white peppercorns
1 oz (25 gm) butter or margarine, melted
1 oz (25 gm) flour
Salt and pepper to taste

1. Put milk into saucepan.
2. Add onion, carrot and celery.
3. Tie mace, parsley, cloves, bay leaf, and peppercorns in a piece of muslin. Add to milk.
4. Slowly bring to boil, stirring.
5. Remove from heat and cover. Leave to stand 45 minutes.
6. Strain into blender. Discard muslin bag and vegetables.
7. Add all remaining ingredients. Run machine until well-blended.
8. Return to saucepan.
9. Cook, stirring continuously, until sauce comes to boil and thickens.
10. Simmer 2 minutes over low heat.

33

CAPER SAUCE

Traditionally served with mutton and skate

½ pint (250 ml) cold milk
1 oz (25 gm) butter or margarine
1 oz (25 gm) flour
1 to 2 tablespoons capers
Salt and pepper to taste

1. Put milk into saucepan with butter or margarine.
2. Heat gently until butter or margarine melts.
3. Pour into blender.
4. Add all remaining ingredients. Run machine just long enough to blend ingredients and coarsely chop capers.
5. Return to saucepan.
6. Cook, stirring continuously, until sauce comes to boil and thickens.
7. Simmer 2 minutes over low heat.

Note

If preferred, sauce may be made with half milk and half mutton or fish stock.

MUSHROOM SAUCE

1 oz (25 gm) butter or margarine
2 oz (50 gm) mushrooms, peeled and sliced
1 oz (25 gm) flour
½ pint (250 ml) cold milk
Salt and pepper to taste

1. Melt butter or margarine in saucepan. Add mushrooms. Fry 3 minutes.
2. Put all remaining ingredients into blender.
3. Run machine until ingredients are well-blended.
4. Pour into saucepan.
5. Cook, stirring continuously, until sauce comes to boil and thickens.
6. Simmer 2 minutes over low heat.

MUSTARD SAUCE

An appetizing sauce to serve with grilled or fried herrings, and cheese and bacon dishes

½ pint (250 ml) cold milk
1 oz (25 gm) butter or margarine

1 oz (25 gm) flour
2 level teaspoons dry mustard
4 teaspoons vinegar
Salt and pepper to taste

1. Put milk into saucepan with butter or margarine.
2. Heat gently until butter or margarine melts.
3. Pour into blender.
4. Add all remaining ingredients. Run machine until ingredients are well-blended.
5. Return to saucepan.
6. Cook, stirring continuously, until sauce comes to boil and thickens.
7. Simmer 2 minutes over low heat.

ONION SAUCE

1 large onion, boiled
½ pint (250 ml) cold milk
1 oz (25 gm) butter or margarine
1 oz (25 gm) flour
¼ level teaspoon grated nutmeg
Salt and pepper to taste

1. Cut onion into quarters.
2. Put milk into saucepan with butter or margarine.
3. Heat gently until butter or margarine melts.
4. Pour into blender.
5. Add onion and all remaining ingredients. Run machine just long enough to blend ingredients and chop onion into fairly fine pieces.
6. Return to saucepan.
7. Cook, stirring continuously, until sauce comes to boil and thickens.
8. Simmer 2 minutes over low heat.

BROWN SAUCE

1½ oz (37 gm) dripping or white cooking fat
1 medium onion, chopped
1 small carrot, sliced
1 small stalk celery, sliced
1 oz (25 gm) mushrooms, chopped
1 oz (25 gm) lean bacon, chopped
1 oz (25 gm) flour
1 pint (approximately ½ litre) water
3 level tablespoons canned or tubed tomato purée
1 bay leaf

BON
FOR COOKING

What is it & why use it?

It is the first ever range of wines which have been specially adapted for cooking, there is:

a Red Wine
a White Wine
and a Cyprus Sherry.

To each of these has been added sufficient wine flavouring to *double the strength of the flavour*. Therefore, the golden rule for cooking is to use half the quantity recommended in your recipe and make up the rest with water.

'Bon for Cooking' comes in small screw capped bottles each of 4¼ fl. oz. which make up to the equivalent of one third of a bottle of ordinary wine or sherry.

We don't presume to tell you why you should buy 'Bon for Cooking' but we can let you know what a panel of 400 housewives thought of it.

Here are some of their most common comments:

'It's a good sized bottle – I've always felt it a waste to buy a full bottle of wine for cooking.'

'It's a cheap way to cook with wine.'

'Nice to be able to use small quantities.'

'No waste and it will keep better in a screw topped bottle.'

'It's nice to have one's own wine just for cooking.'

BON
FOR COOKING

How to use it

With 'Bon for Cooking' you can afford to savour the taste of wine all the time, so why not boldly splash it into everyday dishes like these:

Shepherd's Pie à la Français
1 tbsp Red 'Bon for Cooking' gives Shepherd's Pie a lift.

Steak and Kidney Merci Beaucoup
2 tbsp Red 'Bon for Cooking' makes Steak and Kidney tastier.

Soup Soupçon
$\frac{1}{2}$ glass transforms any soup. Try Red for tomato, White for chicken noodle.

Gravy Très Bien
Stir in 2 tbsp (Red for beef, White for chicken).

Lamb Casserole S'il Vous Plait
Add 1 glass White 'Bon for Cooking' to your stock. Delicious!

Pork Chops Ooh-là-là
Add 1 glass White 'Bon for Cooking' to make chops saucier.

Liver and Onions Au Vin
Pour 1 glass Red 'Bon for Cooking' over your liver for extra flavour.

3 black peppercorns
2 parsley sprigs
1 level teaspoon meat or yeast
  extract
Salt and pepper to taste

1. Melt dripping or cooking fat in heavy saucepan.
2. Add onion, carrot, celery, mushrooms, and bacon.
3. Fry gently, with lid on pan, for 10 minutes, shaking pan frequently.
4. Uncover and continue to fry until vegetables are pale golden.
5. Stir in flour. Cook 2 to 3 minutes, or until flour turns light brown.
6. Gradually blend in water and tomato purée.
7. Tie bay leaf, peppercorns, and parsley in piece of muslin.
8. Add to pan with meat or yeast extract, and salt and pepper to taste.
9. Slowly bring to boil, stirring continuously.
10. Lower heat and cover.
11. Simmer very gently for 1 hour, stirring from time to time.
12. Remove muslin from pan.
13. Pour sauce into blender, half at a time. Run machine until sauce is smooth.
14. Adjust seasoning to taste.
15. Re-heat before serving.

SAUCE BÉARNAISE

A classic sauce to serve with steak

3 tablespoons dry white wine
2 tablespoons tarragon vinegar
1 small onion, finely chopped
2 parsley sprigs
1 dessertspoon warm water
6 oz (150 gm) unsalted butter
3 egg yolks
Salt and pepper to taste
$\frac{1}{4}$ level teaspoon dried tarragon

1. Put wine, tarragon vinegar, onion, and parsley sprigs into small pan.
2. Boil briskly until only 2 tablespoons of liquid remain.
3. Strain. Add warm water. Return to pan and bring gently to boil.
4. Put butter into another saucepan and leave over low heat until it is hot and foamy.

5. Put egg yolks into blender with boiling tarragon liquid.
6. Blend approximately 5 seconds.
7. Remove lid, or small cap in lid, and with machine running at high speed, add hot butter in a thin steady stream. Stop machine.
8. Return cover or cap, and run machine for 30 to 40 seconds, when sauce should be thick and smooth.
9. Season to taste, add dried tarragon, and serve straight away.

Note

1. If sauce is too thick, add 1 or 2 teaspoons hot water.
2. If fresh tarragon is available, chop $\frac{1}{2}$ to 1 teaspoon, and stir into sauce with the seasoning.

BLENDER MAYONNAISE

1 large egg
½ level teaspoon dry or continental mustard
¼ teaspoon Worcestershire sauce
½ level teaspoon salt
Shake of white pepper
¼ level teaspoon sugar
½ pint (250 ml) oil (corn, groundnut, or olive)
2 dessertspoons strained lemon juice
2 dessertspoons wine vinegar
2 dessertspoons boiling water

1. Put egg, mustard, Worcestershire sauce, salt, pepper, sugar, and 4 tablespoons oil into blender.
2. Blend 5 to 6 seconds, or until smooth.
3. Remove lid, or small cap in lid, and with mixer at medium speed, add ¼ pint (125 ml) oil in a slow, steady stream, followed by lemon juice.
4. Cover and blend until thick and smooth.
5. Uncover, and slowly add rest of oil and the vinegar.

6. Blend until completely smooth.
7. Spoon into bowl and stir in boiling water.
8. Transfer to bowl, cover with foil, and refrigerate.

MIXER MAYONNAISE

2 egg yolks
½ level teaspoon dry or continental mustard
½ level teaspoon salt
½ teaspoon Worcestershire sauce
Large pinch of caster sugar
Shake of white pepper
½ pint (250 ml) oil (corn, groundnut, or olive)
2 tablespoons strained lemon juice (or use half lemon juice and half wine vinegar)
1 tablespoon boiling water

1. Put yolks, mustard, salt, Worcestershire sauce, sugar, and pepper into mixer bowl.
2. With mixer at high speed, beat with beaters until smooth and well-blended.
3. Still beating continuously, add oil DROP BY DROP (rapid addition of oil causes mayonnaise to curdle), and continue in this way until the mayonnaise thickens.
4. Stir in half the lemon juice, then continue to beat in oil, a teaspoon at a time.
5. When all the oil has been added and the mayonnaise is thick, stir in rest of lemon juice and boiling water.
6. Transfer to bowl, cover with foil, and refrigerate.

Note

Should mayonnaise curdle, put a fresh egg yolk into bowl, and very gradually beat curdled mayonnaise into it.

BLENDER HOLLANDAISE SAUCE

6 oz (150 gm) unsalted butter
2 tablespoons strained lemon juice
3 egg yolks
Salt and pepper to taste

1. Put butter into a saucepan and leave over a low heat until it is hot and foamy.
2. At the same time, put lemon juice into a small pan and bring to the boil.
3. Put egg yolks into blender with boiling lemon juice.
4. Blend approximately 5 seconds.
5. Remove lid, or small cap in lid, and with machine running at high speed, add hot butter in a thin steady stream. Stop machine.
6. Return cover or cap, and run machine for 30 to 40 seconds, when sauce should be thick and smooth.
7. Season to taste and serve straight away.

Note

If sauce is too thick, add 1 or 2 teaspoons hot water.

ITALIAN STYLE TOMATO SAUCE

1 oz (25 gm) butter or margarine
1 tablespoon salad oil
1 medium onion, chopped
1 celery stalk, chopped
1 garlic clove, chopped (optional)
1 rasher streaky bacon, chopped
1 oz (25 gm) flour
1 can (15 oz or 375 gm approximately) tomatoes
$\frac{1}{2}$ teaspoon Worcestershire sauce
$\frac{1}{4}$ pint (125 ml) water
1 level teaspoon granulated sugar
$\frac{1}{2}$ to 1 level teaspoon salt
1 tablespoon canned or tubed tomato purée
1 bay leaf or oregano to taste

1. Heat butter or margarine, and oil in saucepan.
2. Add onion, celery, garlic (if used), and bacon.
3. Cover pan, and fry slowly until pale gold, shaking pan frequently.
4. Stir in flour and cook 2 minutes.
5. Add all remaining ingredients. Bring to boil, stirring.
6. Lower heat and simmer 30 minutes, stirring frequently.
7. Remove bay leaf, if used.
8. Pour sauce into blender, half at a time. Blend until quite smooth.
9. Return to saucepan, and adjust seasoning to taste.
10. Re-heat before serving.

Note

If sauce is too thick, thin down with a little extra water.

SIMPLE CURRY SAUCE

$\frac{1}{2}$ pint (250 ml) cold milk
1 oz (25 gm) butter or margarine
1 oz (25 gm) flour
2 to 4 level teaspoons curry powder
2 teaspoons lemon juice
2 teaspoons canned or tubed tomato purée
1 level dessertspoon chutney
Salt and pepper to taste

1. Put milk into saucepan with butter or margarine.
2. Heat gently until butter or margarine melts.
3. Pour into blender.
4. Add all remaining ingredients except salt and pepper. Run machine until ingredients are well-blended and smooth.
5. Return to saucepan.
6. Cook, stirring continuously, until sauce comes to boil and thickens.
7. Season to taste with salt and pepper.
8. Simmer 2 minutes over low heat.

HORSERADISH SAUCE

$\frac{1}{4}$ pint (125 ml) double cream
1 tablespoon cold milk
1 level teaspoon icing sugar
3 teaspoons wine vinegar
2 level tablespoons grated horseradish
$\frac{1}{2}$ to 1 level teaspoon salt
Pepper to taste

1. Put cream, milk, and sugar into bowl.
2. With portable or hand-held mixer running at low speed, beat with beaters until stiff.
3. Stir in all remaining ingredients and transfer to small bowl.
4. If not for immediate use, cover closely, and refrigerate.

SAUCE TARTARE

½ pint Blender or Mixer
   Mayonnaise (page 36)
2 level tablespoons gherkins
2 level tablespoons drained capers
2 heaped tablespoons parsley

1. Put mayonnaise into blender.
2. Add all remaining ingredients. Run machine until gherkins, capers, and parsley are finely chopped.
3. Use as required.
4. If not for immediate use, cover with foil, and refrigerate.

MINT SAUCE

1 heaped teacup fresh mint leaves
1 level dessertspoon granulated
   sugar
3 tablespoons malt or wine
   vinegar
2 tablespoons boiling water
½ level teaspoon salt

1. Put all ingredients into blender.
2. Run machine until mint is finely chopped.

APPLE PURÉE SAUCE

1 lb (approximately ½ kilo)
   cooking apples, peeled and
   cored
4 tablespoons water
2 tablespoons granulated sugar
1 oz (25 gm) butter

1. Slice apples into saucepan.
2. Add water and cook gently until soft.
3. Put into blender with sugar and butter. Run machine until sauce is smooth.
4. Re-heat gently before serving, or serve cold.

BREAD SAUCE

2 oz (50 gm) white bread, cubed
4 cloves
1 medium onion, peeled
4 white peppercorns
1 small bay leaf
1 sprig parsley
½ pint (250 ml) milk

½ oz (12 gm) butter or margarine
2 tablespoons single cream
Large pinch of nutmeg
Salt and pepper to taste

1. Put bread cubes, a few at a time, into blender. Run machine until bread is reduced to fine crumbs.
2. Press cloves into onion. Put into saucepan with peppercorns, bay leaf, parsley, and milk.
3. Slowly bring to boil, stirring.
4. Cover and leave over very low heat for 15 minutes. Strain and return to clean pan.
5. Stir in breadcrumbs, butter or margarine, cream, nutmeg, and salt and pepper to taste.
6. Cook gently, stirring continuously, until sauce is smooth and fairly thick.

MELBA SAUCE

12 oz (300 gm) fresh or frozen
   raspberries
1½ level teaspoons arrowroot
1 dessertspoon water
½ teaspoon vanilla essence
2 level tablespoons granulated
   sugar
Red food colouring

1. Put fresh or de-frosted raspberries into blender with arrowroot, water and essence.
2. Add sugar, unless using sweetened frozen raspberries.
3. Blend until smooth.
4. Pour into saucepan and cook slowly, stirring, until mixture comes to the boil.
5. Remove from heat and add a few drops of red food colouring to give a bright red.
6. Serve cold over vanilla ice cream or ice cream and peaches (Peach Melba).

VANILLA SAUCE

½ oz (12 gm) butter
3 level dessertspoons cornflour
½ pint (250 ml) milk
1 level tablespoon granulated
   sugar
1 tablespoon vanilla essence

1. Melt butter in saucepan and keep over low heat.
2. Put all remaining ingredients into blender and blend until smooth.
3. Pour into saucepan with butter.
4. Cook, stirring, until sauce comes to boil and thickens.
5. Simmer 1 minute over low heat.
6. Use with steamed sponge pudding.

BRANDY HARD SAUCE (BRANDY BUTTER)

For Christmas pudding

4 oz (100 gm) unsalted butter, softened
2 oz (50 gm) soft brown sugar
2 oz (50 gm) caster sugar
2 tablespoons brandy
1 oz (25 gm) ground almonds

1. Put butter into mixer bowl.
2. Cream with beaters until very soft.
3. With mixer at low speed, gradually beat in sugar alternately with brandy.
4. Continue beating at medium speed until mixture is light and fluffy in texture.
5. Stir in almonds, then pile into a dish.
6. Refrigerate until firm before serving.

Note

Rum may be substituted for the brandy, and the sauce may be flavoured with ½ level teaspoon cinnamon or mixed spice.

JAM SAUCE

6 level tablespoons jam
2 level teaspoons arrowroot
¼ pint (125 ml) hot water
2 level dessertspoons caster sugar
1 dessertspoon lemon juice
1 inch (2.5 cm) strip of lemon rind

1. Put all ingredients into blender.
2. Blend until smooth and rind is very finely chopped.
3. Pour into saucepan.
4. Slowly bring to boil, stirring continuously.
5. Serve while still hot.
6. Use with steamed sponge pudding.

EGG CUSTARD SAUCE

Serve with fruit or a pudding

2 standard eggs
1 level tablespoon granulated
 sugar
½ pint (250 ml) warm milk
1 teaspoon vanilla essence

1. Put all ingredients into blender and
   blend until smooth.
2. Pour into top of double saucepan,
   or into basin standing over pan of
   gently boiling water.
3. Cook custard, stirring continuously,
   until it thickens sufficiently to coat
   the back of a spoon, but do not
   allow it to boil.
4. Pour into a jug and serve hot or
   cold.

HOT CHOCOLATE FUDGE SAUCE

For ice cream

1 oz (25 gm) butter
2 tablespoons milk
1 tablespoon strong coffee
3 oz (75 gm) soft brown sugar

3 level dessertspoons cocoa
 powder
1 teaspoon vanilla essence
1 teaspoon honey

1. Put butter, milk, and coffee into
   saucepan and bring just up to boil.
2. Pour into blender.
3. Add all remaining ingredients and
   blend until smooth.
4. Return to saucepan and bring
   slowly to the boil.
5. Boil steadily for 5 minutes.
6. Serve straight away.

PEACH AND LEMON SAUCE

1 can (15 oz or 375 gm
 approximately) peach slices
½ teaspoon vanilla essence
2 inch (5 cm) strip lemon rind
2 teaspoons lemon juice

1. Put all ingredients into blender.
2. Blend until smooth and rind is very
   finely chopped.
3. Serve cold over ice cream or, if
   preferred, heat sauce gently, and
   serve hot over steamed or baked
   puddings.

Salad Dressings

FRENCH DRESSING

6 tablespoons salad oil
3 tablespoons wine vinegar or
 lemon juice (or mixture of both)
½ level teaspoon salt
½ level teaspoon dry mustard
½ level teaspoon granulated sugar
¼ teaspoon Worcestershire sauce
Shake of pepper

1. Put all ingredients into blender.
2. Blend until smooth.
3. If not being used immediately,
   pour into screw-top container.
4. Shake before using.

Note

Alternatively, put ingredients into mixer
bowl and beat with beaters until well-
blended.

RAVIGOTE DRESSING

A classic dressing for cold roast meat
salads

6 tablespoons salad oil
3 tablespoons wine vinegar or
 lemon juice (or mixture of both)
1 dessertspoon drained capers
½ small onion, sliced
1 heaped tablespoon parsley
½ level teaspoon salt

$\frac{1}{4}$ level teaspoon sugar
1 or 2 shakes Worcestershire
  sauce
Grinding of black pepper
1 hard-boiled egg, quartered

1. Put oil, vinegar or lemon juice (or
   mixture), capers, onion, parsley,
   salt, sugar, Worcestershire sauce,
   and pepper into blender.
2. Blend until smooth and capers,
   onion, and parsley are chopped.
3. Stop machine and add egg.
4. Blend a few seconds, or until egg
   is chopped.
5. If not being used immediately,
   pour into screw-top container.
6. Shake before using.

TOMATO DRESSING

A useful dressing for all types of salads,
and one which keeps indefinitely in the
refrigerator

1 can (approximately 10 oz or
  250 gm) condensed tomato soup
4 oz (100 gm) granulated sugar
1$\frac{1}{2}$ level teaspoons salt
1 small onion, peeled and
  quartered
$\frac{1}{4}$ pint (125 ml) + 6 tablespoons
  salad oil

$\frac{1}{4}$ pint (125 ml) + 6 tablespoons
  wine vinegar
1 teaspoon Worcestershire sauce
$\frac{1}{2}$ level teaspoon dry mustard

1. Put all ingredients into blender.
2. Blend until smooth and onion is
   very finely chopped.
3. Transfer to air-tight bowl, or put
   into ordinary bowl and cover
   closely with foil.
4. Stir before use.

BLUE VEIN DRESSING

An interesting dressing for green salads

1 oz (25 gm) blue cheese (Danish,
  Gorgonzola, or Stilton)
4 tablespoons salad oil
1 or 2 grindings black pepper
$\frac{1}{2}$ level teaspoon granulated sugar
2 tablespoons wine vinegar
Large pinch of dry mustard
Salt to taste

1. Crumble cheese and put into
   blender.
2. Add all remaining ingredients. Blend
   until smooth.
3. If not being used immediately, pour
   into screw-top container.
4. Shake before using.

SLIMMERS' DRESSING

Oil and sugar are absent, making this tangy dressing less high in calories than the more traditional ones

$\frac{1}{4}$ pint (125 ml) + 5 tablespoons wine, cider vinegar, or lemon juice
4 tablespoons water
3 tablespoons tomato ketchup
2 teaspoons Worcestershire sauce
$\frac{1}{2}$ level teaspoon dry mustard
$\frac{1}{2}$ teaspoon Soy sauce
$\frac{1}{2}$ level teaspoon paprika
Liquid or powdered sugar substitute to taste
1 or 2 shakes garlic or onion salt

1. Put all ingredients into blender.
2. Blend until smooth.
3. Pour into screw-top jar.
4. Shake before using.

CAESAR DRESSING

An American classic for green salads.

1 standard egg
$\frac{1}{4}$ pint (125 ml) salad oil
4 tablespoons lemon juice
4 tablespoons grated Parmesan cheese
1 small onion, sliced
1 level teaspoon salt
$\frac{1}{2}$ level teaspoon made mustard
$\frac{1}{2}$ level teaspoon garlic salt
2 or 3 grindings black pepper
$\frac{1}{2}$ teaspoon Worcestershire sauce

1. Follow method for Slimmers' Dressing.

AVOCADO CREAM DRESSING

A luxurious dressing for all types of salads including egg and poultry

1 medium sized ripe avocado
4 tablespoons soured cream
$\frac{1}{2}$ small onion, sliced
1 teaspoon Worcestershire sauce
$\frac{1}{2}$ level teaspoon salt
$\frac{1}{2}$ level teaspoon garlic salt
$\frac{1}{4}$ pint (125 ml) salad oil
3 tablespoons lemon juice
3 tablespoons wine vinegar

1. Halve avocado. Remove stone and scoop flesh into blender.
2. Add all remaining ingredients.
3. Blend until smooth and onion is very finely chopped.
4. If not being used immediately, put into bowl, cover with foil, and refrigerate.

THOUSAND ISLAND DRESSING

Another American favourite which goes very well with all vegetable salads

$\frac{1}{2}$ pint (250 ml) Mayonnaise (page 36)
1 tablespoon chilli sauce
1 tablespoon sweet pickle
2 oz (50 gm) stuffed olives
1 hard-boiled egg, quartered

4 tablespoons French Dressing
(page 40)
½ level teaspoon onion salt

1. Put all ingredients into blender.
2. Blend until smooth, and olives and egg are finely chopped.
3. If not being used immediately, put into bowl, cover with foil, and refrigerate.
4. Stir before using.

SOURED CREAM AND CURRY DRESSING

Excellent for poultry, egg and rice salads

1 carton (¼ pint or 125 ml) soured cream
1 to 2 level teaspoons curry powder
½ level teaspoon granulated sugar
½ to 1 level teaspoon salt
1 tablespoon milk
1 tablespoon lemon juice
2 inch (5 cm) strip lemon rind

1. Put all ingredients into blender.
2. Blend until smooth and lemon rind is very finely chopped.
3. If not being used immediately, put into bowl, cover with foil, and refrigerate. Stir before using.

Note

Alternatively, finely grate the lemon rind, then put all ingredients into mixer bowl and beat with beaters until well-blended.

CREAM CHEESE AND ONION DRESSING

Excellent with potato salad, over sliced beetroot, with cold poultry, and over hard-boiled eggs

1 packet (3 oz or 75 gm) cream cheese, cubed
2 tablespoons single cream
½ to 1 level teaspoon onion salt
½ level teaspoon paprika
2 tablespoons lemon juice or wine vinegar
½ level teaspoon granulated sugar
Shake of white pepper

1. Put cheese cubes into blender with rest of ingredients.

2. Blend until completely smooth.
3. If not being used immediately, pour into bowl, cover with foil, and refrigerate. Stir before using.

Note

If dressing is too thick, thin down with a little milk.

ITALIAN PIQUANT DRESSING

Suitable for all tossed salads, and salads containing red meat, veal or fish

6 tablespoons salad oil
2 tablespoons lemon juice
2 or 3 grindings of black pepper
1 small garlic clove, peeled and sliced
3 dessertspoons capers
2 level teaspoons granulated sugar
1 teacup parsley, loosely packed
4 anchovy fillets

1. Put all ingredients into blender.
2. Blend until smooth, and garlic, capers, parsley, and anchovies are finely chopped.
3. If not being used immediately, pour into screw-top jar.
4. Shake before using.

COCKTAIL DRESSING

Suitable for all fish cocktails

¼ pint (125 ml) Mayonnaise (page 36)
¼ pint (125 ml) soured cream or natural yogurt
2 level teaspoons bottled horseradish sauce
2 level tablespoons canned or tubed tomato purée
1 teaspoon Worcestershire sauce
1 dessertspoon tomato ketchup
Shake of Tabasco sauce (optional)

1. Put all ingredients into blender.
2. Blend until smooth.
3. If not being used immediately, put into bowl, cover with foil, and refrigerate.
4. Stir before using.

Note

Alternatively, put all ingredients into mixer bowl and beat with beaters until well-blended.

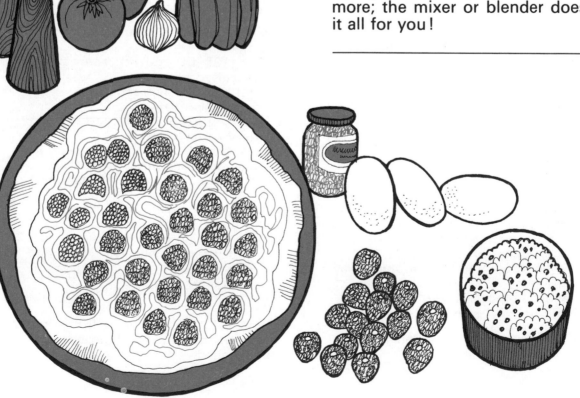

CHAPTER 3

Puddings, Soufflés & Omelets

All tastes have been catered for and whether you are cooking for the 'grand occasion' or simply looking for a treat to please the family, you are sure to find exactly what you want. There are hot and cold puddings of all kinds; high, wide and handsome soufflés; sweet and savoury omelets which are both moist and feather-light and, happy thought, no hard preparation any more; the mixer or blender does it all for you!

Batters

PANCAKES

Makes 7 to 8

$\frac{1}{2}$ pint (250 ml) milk
4 oz (100 gm) plain flour
$\frac{1}{4}$ level teaspoon salt
1 standard egg
1 dessertspoon salad oil
Lemon juice and caster sugar

1. Put all ingredients, except lemon juice and sugar, into blender.
3. Brush base of 8 to 9 inch (20 to 22.5 cm) frying pan with melted white cooking fat.
4. Heat until both pan and fat are hot, but do not allow fat to smoke.
5. Pour sufficient batter into pan to cover base thinly; about 2 to 3 tablespoons.
6. Fry over medium heat until underside is golden.
7. Toss pancake or turn with a fish slice.
8. Fry other side until golden and mottled.
9. Repeat with rest of batter mixture.
10. Sprinkle with lemon juice and caster sugar, and roll up.

Note

1. If preferred, pancakes may be spread with jam or golden syrup.
2. Oil is added to the pancakes to make the texture more velvety.

BLINIS

Continental filled pancakes.
Makes 7 to 8

$\frac{1}{2}$ pint pancake batter
  (see above)
12 oz (300 gm) cottage cheese
1 egg yolk
4 oz (100 gm) caster sugar
1 teaspoon vanilla essence
2 oz (50 gm) seedless raisins
2 oz (50 gm) butter or margarine
1 dessertspoon salad oil
1 level teaspoon cinnamon

1. Cook pancakes on one side only.
2. Put cheese into bowl. Add egg yolk, half the sugar and essence. Mix thoroughly, then stir in raisins.
3. Put equal amounts of cheese mixture on to centres of cooked sides of pancakes.
4. Fold edges of pancakes over filling, envelope-style.
5. Heat butter or margarine, and salad oil in frying pan.
6. When hot but not smoking, put in pancakes with folds underneath.
7. Fry on both sides until golden.
8. Drain on paper towels.
9. Transfer to serving dish and sprinkle with rest of sugar mixed with cinnamon.
10. Serve straight away.

TOAD-IN-THE-HOLE

Serves 4

1 oz (25 gm) dripping or cooking fat
1 lb (approximately $\frac{1}{2}$ kilo) pork sausages
$\frac{1}{2}$ pint (250 ml) milk
4 oz (100 gm) plain flour
$\frac{1}{2}$ level teaspoon salt
1 standard egg

1. Pre-heat oven to hot, 425°F or Gas No. 7 (218°C).
2. Put dripping or fat into tin measuring approximately 10 inches by 12 inches (25 cm by 30 cm).
3. Heat in oven until hot.
4. Prick sausages and add to fat.
5. Bake 10 minutes near top of oven.
6. Put all remaining ingredients into blender. Blend until smooth.
7. Pour into tin over sausages.
8. Bake near top of oven for 30 minutes.
9. Reduce temperature to fairly hot, 400°F or Gas No. 6 (204°C), and bake further 20 to 30 minutes, or until well-risen and golden.
10. Serve with gravy.

YORKSHIRE PUDDING

Serves 4 to 6

2 oz (50 gm) dripping or cooking
  fat
½ pint (250 ml) milk
4 oz (100 gm) plain flour
½ level teaspoon salt
1 standard egg

1. Pre-heat oven to hot, 425°F or Gas No. 7 (218°C).
2. Put dripping or fat into tin measuring approximately 10 inches by 12 inches (25 cm by 30 cm).
3. Heat in oven until hot.
4. Put all remaining ingredients into blender. Blend until smooth.
5. Remove tin from oven and pour in batter.
6. Bake near top of oven for 30 minutes.
7. Reduce temperature to fairly hot, 400°F or Gas No. 6 (204°C), and bake further 20 to 30 minutes, or until well-risen and golden brown.

APPLE BATTER PUDDING

Serves 4

2 oz (50 gm) margarine
1 lb (approximately ½ kilo) cooking apples, peeled and cored
4 oz (100 gm) caster sugar
1 level teaspoon mixed spice
½ pint (250 ml) milk
4 oz (100 gm) plain flour
½ level teaspoon salt
1 standard egg

1. Pre-heat oven to hot, 425°F or Gas No. 7 (218°C).
2. Put margarine into tin measuring approximately 10 inches by 12 inches (25 cm by 30 cm).
3. Heat in oven until hot.
4. Cut apples into fairly thick slices.
5. Remove tin from oven and arrange apples over base. Sprinkle with sugar and spice.
6. Put all remaining ingredients into blender. Blend until smooth.
7. Pour into tin over apples.
8. Bake near top of oven for 30 minutes.
9. Reduce temperature to fairly hot, 400°F or Gas No. 6 (204°C), and bake further 20 to 30 minutes, or until well-risen and golden brown.
10. Serve hot with custard.

RHUBARB OR PLUM BATTER PUDDING

Serves 4

1. Make as above, substituting 1 lb (approximately ½ kilo) rhubarb, cut into 1 inch (2.5 cm) lengths or 1 lb (approximately ½ kilo) stoned plums for the apples.
2. Sprinkle the rhubarb with 1 level teaspoon powdered ginger, or the plums with 1 level teaspoon cinnamon.

COATING BATTER

Suitable for coating fish, meat and vegetables

¼ pint (125 ml) milk
4 oz (100 gm) plain flour
¼ level teaspoon salt
1 standard egg

1. Put all ingredients into blender. Blend until smooth.
2. Use as required.

SAVOURY FRITTER BATTER

A crisp, light batter for coating meat, poultry, fish, and vegetables

4 oz (100 gm) plain flour
½ level teaspoon salt
1 or 2 shakes of white pepper
¼ pint (125 ml) water
1 tablespoon salad oil
2 egg whites

1. Put flour, salt, pepper, water and oil into blender.
2. Blend until smooth.
3. Put egg whites into clean, dry mixer bowl.
4. Beat with beaters until stiff.
5. Fold into flour mixture with a metal spoon.
6. Use straight away.

SWEET FRITTER BATTER

A crisp, light batter suitable for coating

pieces of fruit such as canned pineapple and peaches, or fresh apple rings and pieces of banana.

1. Use same ingredients as Savoury

Fritter Batter, substituting 1 level tablespoon granulated sugar for the white pepper.
2. Follow recipe for Savoury Fritter Batter.

Sweet & Savoury Omelets & Soufflés

PLAIN OMELET

Serves 1

2 standard eggs
2 teaspoons water
Salt and pepper to taste
3 teaspoons butter, unsalted for
  preference

1. Put eggs, water, and salt and pepper into blender.
2. Run machine just long enough to combine yolks and whites smoothly.
3. Melt butter in 6 to 7 inch (15 to 17.5 cm) omelet pan.
4. When hot and sizzling, pour in egg mixture.
5. Using a fork or round-bladed knife, draw edges of omelet mixture towards centre, at the same time tilting pan in all directions to allow any uncooked egg mixture to run to the edges of pan.
6. Cook about ¾ to 1 minute over medium heat, or until underside is golden and top is still moist.
7. Remove from heat and, while omelet is still in pan, fold in half or thirds, and slide on to a plate.
8. Garnish with parsley and serve straight away.

CHEESE OMELET

Serves 1

1. Cut 1 oz (25 gm) dry Cheddar cheese into small cubes.
2. Put into blender. With machine at low speed, blend until cheese is finely chopped.
3. Add eggs, water, and salt and pepper to taste.
4. Run machine just long enough to combine yolks and whites smoothly.
5. Follow recipe for Plain Omelet.

PARSLEY OMELET

Serves 1

1. Put ¼ teacup (or more if preferred) parsley into blender. Run machine until parsley is finely chopped.
2. Add eggs, water, and salt and pepper.
3. Run machine just long enough to combine yolks and whites smoothly.
4. Follow recipe for Plain Omelet.

FILLED OMELETS

Omelets may be filled with freshly fried onions, asparagus tips warmed through in a little butter, freshly fried mushrooms, freshly fried skinned and chopped tomatoes, or chopped cooked chicken warmed through with a little white or Béchamel Sauce (page 33).

1. While omelet is still in the pan, cover one side with filling, then fold over other half.
2. Slide on to a plate and serve straight away.

SPANISH OMELET

Serves 2

$\frac{1}{2}$ medium green pepper, cut into squares
1 medium onion, sliced
4 standard eggs
1 tablespoon water
Salt and pepper to taste
1 oz (25 gm) butter, unsalted for preference
2 teaspoons salad oil
1 large boiled potato, diced
2 medium tomatoes, skinned and chopped

1. Put green pepper and onion into blender.
2. Run machine until both are fairly coarsely chopped. Tip out on to a plate.
3. Put eggs, water, and salt and pepper into blender.
4. Run machine just long enough to blend yolks and whites smoothly.
5. Heat butter and oil in 8 to 9 inch (20 to 22.5 cm) frying pan.
6. Add green pepper, onion and potato. Fry until pale golden.
7. Add tomatoes. Fry a further 5 minutes.
8. Pour in egg mixture, and cook gently until underside is firm and pale golden.
9. Stand below pre-heated hot grill and leave until top is just set.
10. Cut into 2 portions while still in the pan and transfer to 2 warm plates.
11. Serve straight away.

SWEET SOUFFLÉ OMELET

Serves 2

4 standard eggs
1 oz (25 gm) caster sugar
4 teaspoons butter, unsalted for preference
Sifted icing sugar
2 or 3 level tablespoons warmed apricot jam

1. Separate eggs and put whites into mixer bowl.
2. Beat with beaters until stiff.
3. Put yolks and sugar into separate bowl, and beat until thick and almost white in colour.
4. Using a metal spoon, gently fold in beaten whites.
5. Melt butter in large frying pan. When hot and sizzling, spoon in egg mixture.
6. Cook over low heat, without mov-

48

ing mixture at all, for approximately 5 minutes.

7. Remove from heat and stand below pre-heated hot grill. Leave about 3 minutes, or until top is golden and puffy.
8. Turn out on to sheet of greaseproof paper dusted with icing sugar.
9. Score a line down the centre with a knife and cover one side with apricot jam.
10. Fold omelet in half and cut into 2 portions.
11. Serve straight away.

TRADITIONAL CHEESE SOUFFLÉ

Serves 4

3 oz (75 gm) dry Cheddar cheese, cubed
$\frac{1}{4}$ pint (125 ml) cold milk
1 oz (25 gm) butter or margarine
1 oz (25 gm) flour
1 level teaspoon dry mustard
$\frac{1}{2}$ level teaspoon salt
Shake of Cayenne pepper
3 large eggs

1. Pre-heat oven to fairly hot, 375°F or Gas No. 5 (191°C).
2. Put cheese cubes, a few at a time, into blender. Blend on low speed until finely chopped. Tip out on to a plate.
3. Put milk into saucepan with butter or margarine.
4. Heat gently until butter or margarine melts.
5. Pour into blender. Add flour, mustard, salt, and Cayenne pepper.
6. Blend until smooth and return to pan. Cook, stirring continuously, until sauce comes to boil and thickens sufficiently to leave sides of pan clean.
7. Remove from heat and cool 2 minutes.
8. Separate eggs. Put whites into clean, dry mixer bowl. Add yolks to sauce with cheese.
9. Beat egg yolks thoroughly until well mixed.
10. Beat egg whites to a stiff snow with beaters.
11. Using a metal spoon, gently fold into sauce mixture.

12. When evenly combined, transfer to buttered 1$\frac{1}{2}$ pint (approximately $\frac{3}{4}$ litre) soufflé dish, and bake in centre of oven for 45 minutes, until well-risen and golden.
13. Do not open the oven door while the soufflé is cooking. Serve immediately it is ready.

TURKEY OR CHICKEN SOUFFLÉ

Serves 4

$\frac{1}{4}$ pint (125 ml) milk
1 oz (25 gm) butter or margarine
1 oz (25 gm) flour
$\frac{1}{2}$ level teaspoon salt
$\frac{1}{2}$ level teaspoon paprika
Large pinch of nutmeg
Pepper to taste
3 large eggs
4 oz (100 gm) cold cooked turkey or chicken, finely minced

1. Pre-heat oven to fairly hot, 375°F or Gas No. 5 (191°C).
2. Put milk into saucepan with butter or margarine.
3. Heat gently until butter or margarine melts.
4. Pour into blender. Add flour, salt, paprika, nutmeg, and pepper to taste.
5. Blend until smooth and return to pan.
6. Cook, stirring continuously, until sauce comes to boil and thickens sufficiently to leave sides of pan clean.
7. Remove from heat and cool 2 minutes.
8. Separate eggs. Put whites into clean, dry mixer bowl. Add yolks to sauce with turkey or chicken. Beat thoroughly until well-mixed.
9. Beat egg whites to a stiff snow with beaters.
10. Using a metal spoon, fold gently into sauce mixture.
11. When evenly combined, transfer to buttered 1$\frac{1}{2}$ pint (approximately $\frac{3}{4}$ litre) soufflé dish and bake in centre of oven for 45 minutes, until well-risen and golden.
12. Do not open the oven door while the soufflé is cooking. Serve immediately it is ready.

BACON AND MUSHROOM SOUFFLÉ

Serves 4

4 oz (100 gm) mushrooms
2 oz (50 gm) butter or margarine
4 oz (100 gm) boiled bacon
¼ pint (125 ml) cold milk
1 oz (25 gm) flour
1 level teaspoon dry mustard
½ level teaspoon salt
Pepper to taste
3 large eggs

1. Pre-heat oven to fairly hot, 375°F or Gas No. 5 (191°C).
2. Peel, rinse, and slice mushrooms. Gently fry in 1 oz (25 gm) butter or margarine for 4 to 5 minutes. Use to cover base of buttered 2 pint (approximately 1¼ litre) soufflé dish.
3. Chop bacon into tiny cubes.
4. Put milk into saucepan with rest of butter or margarine.
5. Heat gently until butter or margarine melts.
6. Pour into blender. Add flour, mustard, salt, and pepper to taste.
7. Blend until smooth and return to pan. Cook, stirring continuously, until sauce comes to boil and thickens sufficiently to leave sides of pan clean.
8. Remove from heat and cool 2 minutes.
9. Separate eggs. Put whites into clean, dry mixer bowl. Add yolks to sauce with bacon. Beat thoroughly until well mixed.
10. Beat whites to a stiff snow with beaters.
11. Using a metal spoon, gently fold into sauce mixture.
12. When evenly combined, transfer to soufflé dish and bake in centre of oven for 45 minutes, until well-risen and golden.
13. Do not open the oven door while the soufflé is cooking. Serve immediately it is ready.

HOT VANILLA SOUFFLÉ

Serves 4

¼ pint (125 ml) milk
1 oz (25 gm) butter or margarine
1 oz (25 gm) flour
3 large eggs
1 teaspoon vanilla essence
2 oz (50 gm) sugar

1. Pre-heat oven to fairly hot, 375°F or Gas No. 5 (191°C).
2. Put milk into saucepan with butter or margarine.
3. Heat gently until butter or margarine melts.
4. Pour into blender. Add flour. Blend until smooth. Return to saucepan.
5. Cook, stirring continuously, until sauce boils and thickens sufficiently to leave sides of pan clean.
6. Remove from heat and cool 2 minutes.
7. Separate eggs. Put whites into clean, dry mixer bowl. Add yolks to sauce with sugar and essence. Beat thoroughly until well-mixed.
8. Beat whites to a stiff snow.
9. Using a metal spoon, gently fold into sauce mixture.
10. When evenly combined, transfer to buttered 1½ pint (approximately ¾ litre) soufflé dish and bake in centre of oven for 45 minutes, until well-risen and golden.
11. Do not open the oven door while the soufflé is cooking. Serve as soon as it is ready.
12. Serve with single cream or Jam Sauce (page 39).

HOT CHOCOLATE SOUFFLÉ

Follow recipe for Vanilla Soufflé, but melt 2 oz (50 gm) plain chocolate in the milk with the butter or margarine. Serve with single cream.

HOT COFFEE SOUFFLÉ

Follow recipe for Vanilla Soufflé, but dissolve 3 teaspoons instant coffee granules or powder in the milk, and omit vanilla essence. Serve with single cream.

HOT ORANGE OR LEMON SOUFFLÉ

Follow recipe for Vanilla Soufflé, but blend rind of ½ an orange or lemon in the blender until finely chopped, and beat into mixture with sugar and egg yolks. Omit vanilla essence.

COLD CHOCOLATE SOUFFLÉ

Serves 4 to 6

2 oz (50 gm) plain chocolate
3 level teaspoons gelatine
3 tablespoons boiling water
1 teaspoon vanilla essence
2 oz (50 gm) granulated sugar
3 large eggs, separated
¼ pint (125 ml) double cream
1 tablespoon milk

DECORATION

1½ oz (37 gm) shelled walnut
  halves, blanched and toasted
  almonds, or hazelnuts
4 tablespoons double cream
1 dessertspoon milk
1 level teaspoon caster sugar
  (optional)
Crushed flake bar or chocolate
  buttons

1. Put a 4 inch (10 cm) strip of folded greaseproof paper round 1 pint (approximately ½ litre) soufflé dish, making sure that the paper stands 1½ to 2 inches (approximately 3·7 to 5 cm) above edge of dish. Tie firmly to dish with fine string or thick thread.
2. Brush inside of strip with corn oil.
3. Break up chocolate and put into basin standing over pan of hot, but not boiling, water. Leave until melted, stirring once or twice.
4. Put gelatine and boiling water into blender. Blend until gelatine has dissolved. Add chocolate, essence, sugar and egg yolks. Blend until smooth.
5. Put into bowl and leave until *just* beginning to thicken and set.
6. Meanwhile, put egg whites into clean, dry mixer bowl. Beat with beaters until stiff.
7. Beat cream and milk together until softly stiff.
8. With metal spoon, fold egg whites and cream alternately into chocolate mixture.
9. Pour into prepared soufflé dish (mixture should reach almost to top of paper), and refrigerate until firm and set.
10. Remove paper carefully.
11. To decorate, put nuts, a few at a time, into blender. Blend until finely chopped, but do not allow machine to over-run or nuts will become paste-like and oily.
12. Press nuts against sides of soufflé.
13. Beat cream and milk together until thick, adding sugar if liked. Use to decorate top of soufflé, then add crushed flake bar or chocolate buttons.

COLD LEMON SOUFFLÉ

Serves 4 to 6

1 medium lemon
3 level teaspoons gelatine
3 tablespoons boiling water
2 oz (50 gm) granulated sugar
2 large eggs, separated
¼ pint (125 ml) double cream
1 tablespoon milk

DECORATION

1½ oz (37 gm) blanched and
   toasted almonds
4 tablespoons double cream
1 dessertspoon milk
1 level teaspoon caster sugar
   (optional)
Small diamonds cut from angelica,
   or crystallized rose petals

1. Prepare soufflé dish as for Cold Chocolate Soufflé (page 51).
2. Peel lemon thinly. Squeeze out juice and strain.
3. Put lemon rind into blender. Run machine until very finely chopped.
4. Add gelatine and boiling water. Blend until gelatine has dissolved.
5. Add sugar, egg yolks, and lemon juice. Blend until smooth.
6. Pour into bowl and leave until *just* beginning to thicken and set.
7. Meanwhile, put egg whites into clean, dry mixer bowl. Beat with beaters until stiff.
8. Beat cream and milk together until softly stiff.
9. With metal spoon, fold egg whites and cream alternately into lemon mixture.
10. Pour into prepared soufflé dish (mixture should reach almost to top of paper), and refrigerate until firm and set.
11. Before serving, remove paper carefully.
12. To decorate, put nuts, a few at a time, into blender. Blend until finely chopped, but do not allow machine to over-run or nuts will become paste-like and oily.
13. Press nuts against sides of soufflé.
14. Beat cream and milk together until thick, adding sugar if liked. Use to decorate top of soufflé, then add angelica diamonds or rose petals.

COLD ORANGE SOUFFLÉ

Make exactly as Cold Lemon Soufflé, using 1 medium orange instead of the lemon.

Hot & Cold Puddings

ORANGE CREAM SNOW

Serves 4 to 5

1 orange flavour jelly
Boiling water
¼ pint (125 ml) fresh, frozen or
   canned orange juice
¼ pint (125 ml) single cream
2 egg whites
4 glacé cherries, halved
Mint leaves

1. Make up jelly to ½ pint (250 ml) with boiling water. Stir until dissolved. Add orange juice. Pour into mixer bowl.
2. Leave in the cold until *just* beginning to thicken and set.
3. With mixer at medium speed, beat with beaters until foamy, then slowly beat in cream. Transfer to second bowl.
4. Put egg whites into clean, dry mixer bowl.
5. With mixer at high speed, beat with beaters until stiff but not dry.
6. Using metal spoon, fold into jelly mixture.
7. When smooth and evenly combined, transfer to serving bowl.
8. Chill until firm and set.
9. Decorate with cherries and mint.

CHOCOLATE MOUSSE

Serves 4

4 oz (100 gm) plain chocolate
1 oz (25 gm) butter
4 large eggs

DECORATION

Whipped cream
4 hazelnuts

1. Break up chocolate and put into basin standing over saucepan of hot, but not boiling, water. Leave until melted, stirring once or twice.
2. Separate eggs. Beat yolks into chocolate with butter.
3. Put egg whites into clean, dry mixer bowl.
4. With mixer at high speed, beat whites until stiff but not dry.
5. Add chocolate mixture to whites and gently fold in with spatula or metal spoon.
6. When smooth and well-blended, transfer to 4 individual glasses.
7. Chill.
8. Before serving, top each with a whirl of whipped cream and a hazelnut.

MARSHMALLOW BANANA RUM WHIP

Serves 4

4 oz (100 gm) marshmallows
2 tablespoons rum
4 medium bananas
Juice of ½ lemon
¼ pint (125 ml) double cream
1 tablespoon milk
Powdered cinnamon

1. Put marshmallows and rum into saucepan. Stir over low heat until marshmallows have melted.
2. Mash bananas finely, then beat until smooth with the lemon juice.
3. Put cream and milk into mixer bowl. Beat with beaters until thick.
4. Fold into banana mixture alternately with melted marshmallows.
5. Transfer to 4 sundae glasses and chill for about 2 hours.
6. Sprinkle lightly with cinnamon before serving.

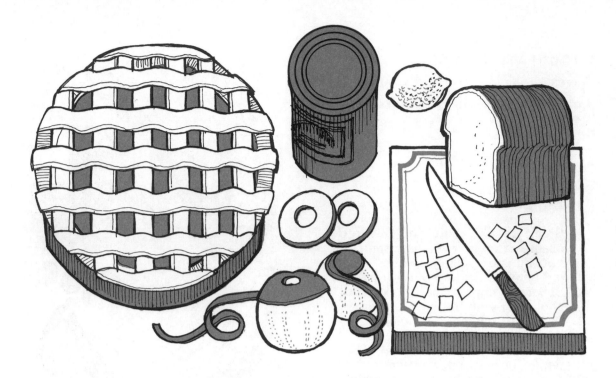

SYRUP TART

Serves 4

6 oz (150 gm) Short Crust Pastry
  (page 63)
2 oz (50 gm) white bread, cubed
Rind of ½ small lemon
2 teaspoons lemon juice
4 level tablespoons golden syrup

1. Pre-heat oven to hot, 425°F or Gas No. 7 (218°C).
2. Roll out pastry thinly and use to line a lightly buttered 8 inch (20 cm) heatproof dish. Trim edges and reserve pastry.
3. Put bread cubes, a few at a time, into blender. Run machine until bread is reduced to fine crumbs. Tip into bowl.
4. Put lemon rind into blender. Run until finely chopped. Add to crumbs with lemon juice and syrup.
5. Mix thoroughly, then spread over base of pastry. Moisten edge of pastry round plate with water.
6. Roll out rest of pastry and cut into thin strips.
7. Arrange over filling in trellis design.
8. Press well on to pastry round edge of plate.
9. Bake just above centre of oven for 20 to 30 minutes, or until golden.
10. Serve with single cream or custard.

BUTTERED APPLE CHARLOTTE

Serves 4 to 6

4 oz (100 gm) white bread, cubed
Rind of 1 lemon
½ to 1 level teaspoon powdered
  cinnamon (optional)
4 oz (100 gm) Demerara sugar
1½ lb (approximately ¾ kilo)
  cooking apples
4 oz (100 gm) melted butter

1. Pre-heat oven to moderate, 350°F or Gas No. 4 (177°C).
2. Put bread cubes, a few at a time, into blender.
3. Run machine until bread is reduced to fine crumbs. Tip into bowl.
4. Put rind into blender. Run machine until finely chopped. Add to crumbs with cinnamon (if used) and sugar. Toss well to mix.
5. Peel, core, and thinly slice apples.
6. Fill buttered 2½ pint (approximately 1½ litre) heatproof dish with alternate layers of crumb mixture and apples, beginning and ending with crumb mixture, and sprinkling melted butter between layers.
7. Put into centre of oven and bake for 45 minutes, or until apples are soft and top layer of crumb mixture is crisp and golden.
8. Serve hot with cream or custard.

54

LEMON MERINGUE PIE

Serves 4 to 6

**4 oz (100 gm) Short Crust Pastry
(page 63)**

FILLING

**¼ pint (125 ml) cold water
3 level tablespoons cornflour
3 oz (75 gm) caster sugar
2 large lemons
2 yolks from large eggs
1 heaped teaspoon butter**

MERINGUE TOPPING

**2 whites from large eggs
3 oz (75 gm) caster sugar**

1. Pre-heat oven to hot, 425°F or Gas No. 7 (218°C).
2. Stand 7 inch (17.5 cm) flan ring on lightly greased baking tray.
3. Roll out pastry thinly and use to line flan ring.
4. Trim edges, then prick all over lightly with a fork.
5. Line base and sides with a piece of aluminium foil to prevent pastry from rising as it cooks.
6. Bake towards top of oven for 15 minutes. Remove from oven. Carefully lift out foil, then return pastry case to oven for 10 minutes, or until golden.
7. Remove flan ring. Leave pastry case on baking tray while preparing filling. Reduce oven temperature to cool, 300°F or Gas No. 2 (149°C).
8. Put water, cornflour and sugar into blender.
9. Peel lemons very thinly. Add rind to blender.
10. Squeeze lemons. Add juice to blender.
11. Run machine until lemon rind is very finely chopped.
12. Pour into saucepan. Cook, stirring continuously, until mixture comes to boil and thickens. Simmer 2 minutes.
13. Remove from heat, and beat in egg yolks and butter. Pour into flan case.
14. To make meringue topping, put egg whites into clean, dry mixer bowl and beat with beaters until stiff.
15. Add 2 oz (50 gm) caster sugar. Continue beating until meringue is very stiff and stands in shiny, firm peaks.
16. With metal spoon, fold in rest of sugar.
17. Pile over lemon filling and cook in centre of oven for 35 to 45 minutes, or until meringue is very pale golden and crisp.
18. Serve hot or cold.

PEAR AND CHOCOLATE UPSIDE DOWN PUDDING

Serves 4

**1 can (approximately 15 oz or 375 gm) pear halves
1 tablespoon soft brown sugar
5 oz (125 gm) self-raising flour
1 oz (25 gm) cocoa powder
3 oz (75 gm) softened butter or margarine
3 oz (75 gm) soft brown sugar
1 teaspoon vanilla essence
2 standard eggs
3 tablespoons cold milk**

1. Pre-heat oven to moderate, 350°F or Gas No. 4 (177°C).
2. Drain pears (syrup from can may be used for cold drinks).
3. Sprinkle 1 tablespoon of sugar over base of buttered 2 pint (approximately 1½ litre) heatproof dish. Arrange pear halves on top, cut sides down.
4. Sift flour and cocoa on to a plate.
5. Put butter or margarine with sugar and essence into mixer bowl.
6. Cream with beaters until mixture is light and fluffy in texture.
7. Beat in whole eggs, one at a time, adding tablespoon of sifted dry ingredients with each.
8. Using metal spoon, gently fold in rest of dry ingredients alternately with milk.
9. When smooth and evenly combined, transfer to prepared dish, spreading top evenly with a knife.
10. Bake in centre of oven for 50 minutes to 1 hour or until wooden cocktail stick, inserted into centre of pudding, comes out clean.
11. Turn out on to a warm plate and accompany with cream or custard.

55

FRUIT FOOL

Serves 4

1 lb (approximately ½ kilo) rhubarb, cooking apples, or gooseberries
6 oz (150 gm) granulated sugar
2 tablespoons water
½ pint (250 ml) freshly made sweetened custard
Red or green food colouring
4 heaped teaspoons whipped or clotted cream
2 glacé cherries, halved

1. Prepare fruit according to type. Cut rhubarb into 2 inch lengths; peel and thinly slice apples; top and tail gooseberries.
2. Put fruit into saucepan with sugar and water. Cook gently until fruit is soft.
3. Cool slightly, then put into blender. Run machine until smooth.
4. Stir fruit purée into custard and colour pale pink for rhubarb, or pale green for apples or gooseberries.
5. Transfer to 4 sundae glasses and chill.
6. Before serving, top each with cream and half a cherry.

Note

To make a richer Fool, stir the fruit purée (which should be completely cold) into ½ pint (250 ml) lightly sweetened whipped cream.

APPLE AND BLACKBERRY CRUNCHY CRUMBLE

8 oz (200 gm) cooking apples, peeled, cored, and sliced
8 oz (200 gm) blackberries
2 tablespoons water
3 oz (75 gm) granulated sugar

TOPPING

4 oz (100 gm) plain flour
1 level teaspoon cinnamon
2 oz (50 gm) butter
2 oz (50 gm) soft brown sugar
2 level tablespoons desiccated coconut
2 level tablespoons rolled oats

1. Pre-heat oven to warm, 325°F or Gas No. 3 (163°C).
2. Put apples into buttered 1½ pint (¾ litre) heatproof dish with blackberries, water and granulated sugar.
3. Sift flour and cinnamon into mixer bowl.
4. Cut butter into small pieces and add to flour mixture.
5. With mixer at low speed, run beaters through ingredients until they resemble fine breadcrumbs.
6. Add sugar, coconut and oats, and toss ingredients lightly together to mix.
7. Sprinkle thickly over fruit.
8. Stand dish on baking tray and cook in centre of oven for 45 minutes to 1 hour, or until fruit is tender and top is pale golden.
9. Serve warm with cream or custard.

STRAWBERRY SHORTCAKES

Serves 4

8 oz (200 gm) self-raising flour
1 level teaspoon baking powder
½ level teaspoon salt
2 level tablespoons caster sugar
2 oz (50 gm) butter or margarine
1 standard egg
Cold milk
Extra milk or a little beaten egg for brushing

FILLING

Butter
8 to 12 oz (200 to 300 gm) fresh strawberries, sliced
Icing sugar

TOPPING

4 heaped teaspoons whipped or clotted cream
Icing sugar

1. Pre-heat oven to very hot, 450°F or Gas No. 8 (232°C).
2. Sift flour, baking powder, salt and sugar into mixer bowl.
3. Cut butter or margarine into small pieces and add to flour mixture.
4. With mixer at low speed, run beaters through ingredients until they resemble fine breadcrumbs.
5. Break egg into measuring cup. Make up to ¼ pint (125 ml) with cold milk. Beat well together with fork.

6. Add all at once to flour mixture. Using a knife, mix to soft dough.
7. Turn out on to floured surface and knead lightly until smooth.
8. Roll out to 1 inch in thickness and cut into 4 rounds with a 3½ to 4 inch (9 to 10 cm) cutter.
9. Transfer to greased baking tray and brush tops with milk or egg.
10. Bake near top of oven for 15 to 20 minutes, or until well-risen and golden.
11. Transfer to wire cooling rack.
12. When lukewarm, gently break each Shortcake in half with fingers and spread thickly with butter.
13. Sandwich together with strawberry slices, reserving a few for decoration.
14. Top each with cream and strawberries, then dredge with icing sugar.
15. Serve straight away.

RASPBERRY CREAM PAVLOVA

3 egg whites
Pinch of cream of tartar
6 oz (150 gm) caster sugar
1 level teaspoon cornflour
1 teaspoon vinegar
¼ pint (250 ml) double cream
1 tablespoon milk
8 oz (200 gm) fresh raspberries
Icing sugar

1. Pre-heat oven to cool, 300°F or Gas No. 2 (149°C).
2. Cover large baking tray with silicone treated paper.
3. Put egg whites and cream of tartar into clean, dry mixer bowl.
4. Beat with beaters until very stiff.
5. Add half the sugar. Continue beating until meringue is very shiny and stands in high peaks.
6. Using a metal spoon, fold in remaining sugar with cornflour and vinegar.
7. Transfer to prepared baking tray, spreading meringue mixture into an 8 inch (20 cm) round.
8. Put into centre of oven and cook for 1¼ to 1½ hours, or until Pavlova is pale golden and crisp on the outside and soft inside.
9. Switch off heat and leave Pavlova

in the oven until completely cold.
10. Lift away from paper and transfer to serving dish.
11. Put cream and milk into mixer bowl, and beat with beaters until thick.
12. Pile over Pavlova, then stud with raspberries.
13. Sift icing sugar lightly over the top.

CHRISTMAS PUDDING

Makes 3 or 4

**Rind and juice of 1 small lemon
and 1 small orange**
**12 oz (approximately 300 gm)
white bread, cubed**
**12 oz (approximately 300 gm)
plain flour**
1 level teaspoon salt
2 level teaspoons mixed spice
1 level teaspoon cinnamon
1 level teaspoon powdered ginger
12 oz (300 gm) soft brown sugar
**12 oz (300 gm) finely shredded
suet**
3 lb (1½ kilos) mixed dried fruit
8 oz (200 gm) mixed chopped peel
**4 oz (100 gm) shelled walnut
halves**
4 oz (100 gm) blanched almonds
1 tablespoon black treacle
3 tablespoons brandy
4 standard eggs, fork-beaten
Milk to mix

1. Brush four 2 pint (approximately 1¼ litre) or three 3 pint (1¾ litre) basins thickly with melted cooking fat.
2. Put lemon and orange rind into blender. Run machine until finely chopped. Tip into very large mixing bowl.
3. Put bread cubes, a few at a time, into blender. Run machine until bread is reduced to fine crumbs. Add to mixing bowl.
4. Sift flour, salt, spice, cinnamon, and ginger into bowl over crumbs.
5. Add sugar, suet, dried fruit, and peel.
6. Coarsely chop walnuts and almonds, and add to crumb mixture. Toss ingredients well together.
7. Stirring thoroughly, mix to a soft dropping consistency with treacle, brandy, eggs, and milk.
8. Cover loosely and leave mixture to stand for approximately 4 hours in the cool.

9. Stir again, then transfer equal amounts to prepared basins.
10. Cover tops, first with a double thickness of greased greaseproof paper, and then with a double thickness of aluminium foil.
11. Steam the 2 pint (1¼ litre) basins for 8 hours and the larger ones for 10, topping up pans with extra boiling water as and when necessary.
12. Leave in basin for ½ an hour before turning out.
13. Wrap each pudding in a double thickness of greaseproof paper and then in a clean cloth.
14. Store in a cool, dry place for at least 1 month to mature before using.
15. Re-steam each pudding for approximately 3 hours before serving.

STEAMED FRUITED CRUMB PUDDING

Serves 4

4 oz (100 gm) white bread, diced
4 oz (100 gm) plain flour
1½ level teaspoons baking powder
1 level teaspoon mixed spice
Pinch of salt
3 oz (75 gm) caster or soft brown sugar
3 oz (75 gm) finely shredded suet
4 oz (100 gm) mixed dried fruit
1 large egg, fork-beaten
Milk to mix

1. Put bread dice, a few at a time, into blender. Run machine until bread is reduced to fine crumbs.
2. Sift flour, baking powder, spice, and salt into bowl.
3. Add crumbs, sugar, suet, and fruit.
4. Using a fork, stir in egg and sufficient milk to give a soft dropping consistency.
5. Transfer to greased 2 pint (1¼ litre) pudding basin.
6. Cover with double thickness of greased greaseproof paper or aluminium foil.
7. Steam steadily for 2½ to 3 hours, topping up saucepan with extra boiling water as and when necessary.
8. Turn out and serve with custard.

STEAMED SPONGE JAM PUDDING

2 tablespoons raspberry or strawberry jam
5 oz (125 ml) self-raising flour
Pinch of salt
4 oz (100 gm) softened butter or margarine
4 oz (100 gm) caster sugar
½ teaspoon vanilla essence
2 standard eggs
2 tablespoons cold milk

1. Brush 2 pint (approximately 1¼ litre) pudding basin with butter.
2. Put jam into base of basin.
3. Sift flour and salt on to a plate.
4. Put butter or margarine with sugar and essence into mixer bowl. Cream with beaters until mixture is light and fluffy in texture.
5. Beat in whole eggs, one at a time, adding a tablespoon of sifted flour with each.
6. Using a metal spoon, gently fold in rest of flour alternately with milk.
7. When evenly combined, transfer to prepared basin.
8. Cover top with double thickness of greased greaseproof paper or aluminium foil.
9. Steam steadily for 1½ to 2 hours, or until well-risen and firm.
10. Turn out on to a warm dish and serve with custard or single cream.

ORANGE SORBET

Serves 6 to 8

6 oz (150 gm) granulated sugar
¾ pint (375 ml) water
Juice of 1 lemon
Rind and juice of 1 orange
3 tablespoons golden syrup,
  slightly warmed
1 egg white
3 level dessertspoons caster sugar

1. Set refrigerator control to coldest setting.
2. Wash and dry 2 ice cube trays.
3. Put sugar and water into saucepan. Leave over very low heat until dissolved.
4. Add lemon and orange juice.
5. Put orange rind into blender. Run machine until finely chopped.
6. Add to orange mixture with syrup.
7. Stir well to mix, then leave until completely cold.
8. Pour into trays and leave in freezing compartment of refrigerator for 1 hour.
9. Remove trays from freezing compartment.
10. Put egg white into clean, dry mixer bowl. Beat with beaters until stiff. Add sugar and continue beating until meringue is very shiny and stands in high, firm peaks.
11. Put orange mixture into bowl and beat well with a fork.
12. Gradually stir in beaten egg white.
13. Return to trays and chill 45 minutes.
14. Tip into mixer bowl. Beat with beaters until smooth and well-blended.
15. Return to trays and freeze until firm; 1½ to 2 hours.
16. Spoon into small glasses and serve straight away.

QUEEN OF PUDDINGS

Serves 4

3 oz (75 gm) white bread
Rind of ½ small lemon
1 oz (25 gm) caster sugar
¾ pint (375 ml) milk
1 oz (25 gm) butter
2 egg yolks
2 tablespoons warmed raspberry or apricot jam

TOPPING

2 egg whites
3 oz (75 gm) caster sugar

1. Pre-heat oven to moderate, 350°F or Gas No. 4 (177°C).
2. Put bread cubes, a few at a time, into blender. Run machine until bread is reduced to fine crumbs. Tip into bowl.
3. Add lemon rind to blender. Run machine until finely chopped. Add to crumbs.
4. Add sugar and toss ingredients lightly together to mix.
5. Put milk and butter into saucepan. Leave over low heat until butter melts.
6. Stir into crumb mixture. Leave to stand 30 minutes.
7. Beat in egg yolks and transfer to buttered 1½ pint (approximately ¾ litre) pie dish.
8. Bake in centre of oven for 30 minutes, or until set.
9. Spread with jam.
10. Put egg whites into clean, dry mixer bowl.
11. Beat with beaters until stiff.
12. Add half the sugar. Continue beating until meringue is very shiny and stands in firm peaks. Using metal spoon, fold in rest of sugar.
13. Pile over jam, swirling meringue with a fork.
14. Return to centre of oven and cook for a further 30 minutes.
15. Serve hot with single cream.

ZABAGLIONE

Serves 4

4 egg yolks
4 tablespoons caster sugar
4 tablespoons Marsala

1. Stand basin over saucepan of hot, but not boiling, water.
2. Put in egg yolks, sugar and Marsala.
3. With portable or hand-held mixer, beat with beaters until mixture is very thick, pale in colour, and has trebled in bulk.
4. Pour into 4 glasses and serve straight away with crisp biscuits.

CHOCOLATE WHISKY CREAM

Serves 4

2 level tablespoons cocoa powder
2 tablespoons boiling water
1 tablespoon whisky
3 standard eggs, separated
3 oz (75 gm) caster sugar
½ pint (250 ml) double cream
Chocolate vermicelli for decoration

1. Blend cocoa and boiling water well together. Stir in whisky.
2. Put egg yolks and sugar into mixer bowl.
3. Beat with beaters until thick and pale in colour. With mixer at low speed, gradually beat in cocoa mixture. Transfer to second bowl.
4. Put egg whites in clean, dry mixer bowl. Beat to a stiff snow with beaters.
5. Whip cream until thick, then gently stir in cocoa mixture.
6. Using a metal spoon, lightly fold in egg whites.
7. When smooth and evenly combined, transfer to 4 large wine-type glasses.
8. Chill for 30 minutes.
9. Sprinkle with chocolate vermicelli and serve with wafer biscuits.

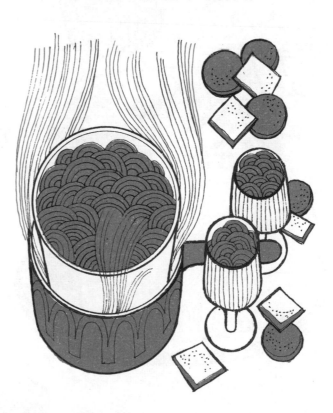

CHAPTER 4

Baking

There is nothing quite as welcoming as the appetizing smell of home-baked cakes and bread, and for those of you who are enthusiastic bakers and take pride in producing your own goodies, the following recipes for mixer-made cakes, buns (with appropriate fillings and icings), biscuits, scones and bread should give you plenty of scope for your talent without involving you in all those arm-aching and time-consuming chores: creaming, whisking, beating, kneading and rubbing-in.

Pastry, Biscuits & Scones

SHORT CRUST PASTRY

4 oz (100 gm) plain flour
¼ level teaspoon salt
1 oz (25 gm) butter or margarine
1 oz (25 gm) white cooking fat
  or lard
Approximately 1 tablespoon cold
  water to mix

1. Sift flour and salt into mixer bowl.
2. Cut butter or margarine, and cooking fat or lard into small pieces. Add to flour.
3. With mixer at low speed, run beaters through ingredients until they resemble fine breadcrumbs.
4. Using a fork, mix to a stiff paste with water.
5. Turn out on to lightly floured surface and knead until smooth.
6. Use as required.

CHEESE PASTRY

4 oz (100 gm) plain flour
¼ level teaspoon *each*, salt and dry
  mustard
1 oz (25 gm) butter or margarine
1 oz (25 gm) white cooking fat
  or lard
2 oz (50 gm) Cheddar cheese, very
  finely grated
Cayenne pepper
1 egg yolk
Cold water

1. Sift flour, salt and mustard into mixer bowl.
2. Cut butter or margarine, and cooking fat or lard into small pieces. Add to flour.
3. With mixer at low speed, run beaters through ingredients until they resemble fine breadcrumbs.
4. Add cheese and one or two shakes of Cayenne pepper, and toss ingredients lightly together with fingertips.
5. Using a fork, mix to a stiff paste with the egg yolk and 1 or 2 teaspoons cold water.
6. Knead lightly until smooth on floured surface.
7. Wrap in foil.
8. Refrigerate about 1 hour before rolling out and using.

MACAROONS

Makes 10

2 egg whites
4 oz (100 gm) ground almonds
8 oz (200 gm) caster sugar
½ oz (12 gm) fine semolina
1 teaspoon *each* almond and
  vanilla essence
1 oz (25 gm) flaked almonds
A little extra egg white for
  brushing

1. Pre-heat oven to warm, 325°F or Gas No. 3 (163°C).
2. Brush 2 baking trays with oil, then line with rice paper.
3. Put a ½ inch plain icing pipe into a forcing bag.
4. Put egg whites into clean, dry mixer bowl.
5. With mixer at high speed, beat with beaters until whites are foamy but not stiff.
6. Reduce speed to low and gradually add almonds, sugar, semolina, and essences.
7. Continue beating for about 3 to 5 minutes.
8. Transfer to forcing bag and pipe approximately 10 small mounds, well apart on each tray.
9. Sprinkle with flaked almonds, then brush with egg white.
10. Bake in centre of oven for 20 to 25 minutes, or until pale golden.
11. Leave on trays 5 minutes.
12. Carefully lift off Macaroons, removing rice paper round edges of each.
13. Cool on a wire rack and store in an air-tight tin when cold.

FLAKY PASTRY

8 oz (200 gm) plain flour
1 level teaspoon salt
3 oz (75 gm) butter or margarine
3 oz (75 gm) white cooking fat
  or lard
¼ pint (125 ml) ice cold water
1 teaspoon lemon juice

1. Sift flour and salt into mixer bowl.
2. Cut 1½ oz (37 gm) mixture of butter or margarine, and cooking fat or lard into small pieces. Add to flour.
3. With mixer at low speed, run beaters through ingredients until they resemble fine breadcrumbs.
4. Using a fork, mix to a soft dough with water and lemon juice.
5. Turn out on to floured surface and knead lightly until smooth.
6. Roll out into rectangle measuring 18 inches by 6 inches (45 cm by 15 cm).
7. Starting from the top edge (the edge furthest away from you), cover two-thirds of the pastry with small flakes of butter or margarine, and cooking fat or lard, using about one-third of the total amount left (1½ oz or 37 gm).
8. Sprinkle with flour, then fold pastry into three, envelope style, by bringing the lower third (the piece nearest to you) over centre, and then folding the top third over.
9. Press edges lightly together with a rolling pin to seal.
10. Wrap in foil or put into a polythene bag, and refrigerate for 30 minutes.
11. Unwrap, and with folded edges to the left and right roll out into a rectangle 18 inches by 6 inches (45 cm by 15 cm).
12. Cover with another 1½ oz (37 gm) of butter or margarine, and cooking fat or lard as before.
13. Sprinkle with flour, fold up, seal edges, wrap, and refrigerate.
14. Repeat once more, using up rest of butter or margarine, and cooking fat or lard. Refrigerate a further 30 minutes.
15. Re-roll into same size rectangle, then fold in three and chill about 45 minutes.
16. Roll out to about ¼ inch and use.

SHORTBREAD

Makes 8

2 oz (50 gm) caster sugar
4 oz (100 gm) softened butter
6 oz (150 gm) plain flour, sifted

1. Pre-heat oven to warm, 325 °F or Gas No. 3 (163 °C).
2. Put sugar and butter into mixer bowl. Cream with beaters until mixture is light and fluffy in texture.
3. Using a fork, stir in flour and continue stirring until well-mixed but still crumbly.
4. Transfer to 7 inch (17·5 cm) sandwich tin and press lightly with fingertips until mixture is spread evenly over tin.
5. Ridge edge with a fork, then prick rest of Shortbread all over.
6. Bake in centre of oven until the colour of pale straw, about 45 minutes.
7. Leave until lukewarm, then cut into 8 wedges with a sharp knife.
8. Cool on a wire rack.
9. Store in an air-tight tin when cold.

WALNUT REFRIGERATOR BISCUITS

Makes 25

2 oz (50 gm) shelled walnut
  halves
6 oz (150 gm) self-raising flour
Pinch of salt
3 oz (75 gm) softened butter or
  margarine
3 oz (75 gm) soft brown sugar
1 teaspoon vanilla essence
1 standard egg

1. Put nuts, a few at a time, into blender. Run machine until nuts are finely chopped, but do not allow machine to over-run or nuts will become paste-like and oily.
2. Sift flour and salt on to a plate.
3. Put butter or margarine with sugar and essence into mixer bowl.
4. Cream with beaters until light and fluffy in texture. Beat in egg.
5. Using a fork, stir in ground nuts, followed by flour.
6. Turn mixture out on to a floured surface and shape into a long roll

of about 1½ to 2 inches in diameter.

7. Wrap in foil and refrigerate for a minimum of 6 hours.
8. Unwrap and cut into about 25 slices.
9. Stand, well apart, on greased baking trays.
10. Bake in centre of fairly hot oven, 375°F or Gas No. 5 (191°C), for about 12 minutes, or until golden.
11. Carefully lift biscuits off trays and cool on wire racks.
12. Store in an air-tight tin when cold.

FLAPJACKS

Makes 16

4 oz (100 gm) softened butter or margarine
2 oz (50 gm) soft brown sugar
2 oz (50 gm) golden syrup, warmed
8 oz (200 gm) rolled oats

1. Pre-heat oven to fairly hot, 375°F or Gas No. 5 (191°C).
2. Brush 10 inch by 8 inch (25 cm by 20 cm) shallow tin with melted butter.
3. Put butter or margarine with sugar and syrup into mixer bowl.
4. Cream with beaters until light and fluffy in texture.
5. Using a fork, stir in rolled oats.
6. Spread mixture into prepared tin.
7. Bake in centre of oven for 30 minutes.
8. Leave to stand for 5 minutes, then cut into approximately 16 fingers.
9. Cool on a wire rack and store in an air-tight tin when cold.

COCONUT COOKIES

Makes 20

4 oz (100 gm) plain flour
Pinch of salt
4 oz (100 gm) softened butter or margarine
2 oz (50 gm) caster sugar
1 teaspoon vanilla essence
½ oz (12 gm) desiccated coconut
10 glacé cherries, halved

1. Pre-heat oven to fairly hot, 375°F of Gas No. 5 (191°C).
2. Sift flour and salt on to a plate.

3. Put butter or margarine with sugar and essence into mixer bowl.
4. Cream with beaters until light and fluffy in texture.
5. Using a fork, stir in flour and coconut.
6. Put 20 equal amounts of mixture well apart on two buttered baking trays.
7. Flatten slightly with prongs of a fork dipped in caster sugar.
8. Top each with half a glacé cherry.
9. Bake in centre of oven for 15 minutes, or until pale golden.
10. Leave on trays for 5 minutes, then transfer to wire cooling rack.
11. Store in an air-tight tin when cold.

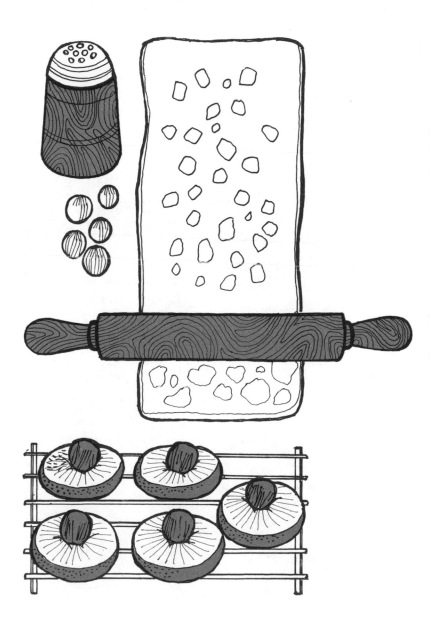

PLAIN SCONES

Makes 10

8 oz (200 gm) self-raising flour
1 level teaspoon salt
2 oz (50 gm) butter or margarine
¼ pint (125 ml) cold milk
Extra milk or a little beaten egg
for brushing

1. Pre-heat oven to very hot, 450°F or Gas No. 8 (232°C).
2. Sift flour and salt into mixer bowl.
3. Cut butter or margarine into small pieces and add to flour.
4. With mixer at low speed, run beaters through ingredients until they resemble fine breadcrumbs.
5. Add milk all at once.
6. Using a knife, mix to a soft dough.
7. Turn out on to floured surface and knead lightly until smooth.
8. Roll out to ½ inch in thickness.
9. Cut into approximately 10 rounds with 2½ inch (6.2 cm) plain or fluted biscuit cutter dipped in flour.
10. Transfer to greased baking tray and brush tops with milk or egg.
11. Bake near top of oven for 7 to 10 minutes or until well-risen and golden.
12. Cool on a wire rack.

Note

If preferred, use plain flour with 3 level teaspoons baking powder.

SWEET TEA SCONES

Makes 10

8 oz (200 gm) self-raising flour
1 level teaspoon salt
1 to 2 level tablespoons caster
sugar
2 oz (50 gm) butter or margarine
¼ pint (125 ml) cold milk
Extra milk or a little beaten egg
for brushing

1. Pre-heat oven to very hot, 450°F or Gas No. 8 (232°C).
2. Sift flour, salt and sugar into mixer bowl.
3. Cut butter or margarine into small pieces and add to flour mixture.
4. With mixer at low speed, run beaters through ingredients until they resemble fine breadcrumbs.
5. Add milk all at once.
6. Using a knife, mix to soft dough.
7. Turn out on to floured surface and knead lightly until smooth.
8. Roll out to ½ inch in thickness.
9. Cut into approximately 10 rounds with 2½ inch (6.2 cm) plain or fluted biscuit cutter dipped in flour.
10. Transfer to greased baking tray and brush tops with milk or egg.
11. Bake near top of oven for 7 to 10 minutes, or until well-risen and golden.
12. Cool on a wire rack.

Note

1. If preferred, use plain flour with

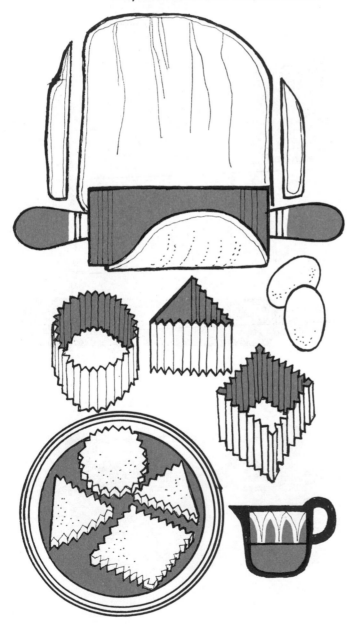

3 level teaspoons baking powder.
2. For smaller scones, cut into about 16 rounds with 2 inch (5 cm) cutter.

CHEESE SCONES

Makes 10

8 oz (200 gm) self-raising flour
1 level teaspoon salt
1 level teaspoon dried mustard
Shake of pepper
2 oz (50 gm) butter or margarine
2 oz (50 gm) dry Cheddar cheese, finely grated
$\frac{1}{4}$ pint (125 ml) cold milk
Extra milk or a little beaten egg for brushing

1. Pre-heat oven to very hot, 450°F or Gas No. 8 (232°C).
2. Sift flour, salt, mustard and pepper into mixer bowl.
3. Cut butter or margarine into small pieces and add to flour mixture.
4. With mixer at low speed, run beaters through ingredients until they resemble fine breadcrumbs.
5. Add cheese and toss ingredients lightly together to mix.
6. Add milk all at once.
7. Using a knife, mix to a soft dough.
8. Turn out on to floured surface and knead lightly until smooth.
9. Roll out to $\frac{1}{2}$ inch in thickness.
10. Cut into approximately 10 rounds with 2$\frac{1}{2}$ inch (6.2 cm) plain or fluted biscuit cutter dipped in flour.
11. Transfer to greased baking tray and brush tops with milk or egg.
12. Bake near top of oven for 7 to 10 minutes, or until well-risen and golden.
13. Cool on a wire rack.

Note

If preferred, use plain flour with 3 level teaspoons baking powder.

DROPPED SCONES OR SCOTCH PANCAKES

Makes 10

4 oz (100 gm) self-raising flour
Pinch of salt
1 tablespoon caster sugar
1 dessertspoon salad oil
$\frac{1}{4}$ pint (125 ml) cold milk

1. Sift flour and salt on to plate. Transfer to blender.
2. Add all remaining ingredients.
3. With blender at high speed, run machine until batter is smooth.
4. Brush a heavy-based frying pan, solid electric hot plate or griddle with melted fat.
5. Heat until hot, but do not allow fat to over-heat and smoke.
6. Drop dessertspoons of batter, from the tip of the spoon, into pan or on to hot plate or griddle, allowing a little room between each for spreading.
7. Cook until bubbles rise to the surface and break, and the undersides are golden.
8. Turn over with a slice or broad-bladed knife and cook until golden.
9. Stack scones, as they are cooked, in folded tea towel to keep warm and moist.
10. Serve with butter or thick whipped cream, and jam, syrup or honey.

Large & Small Cakes

PLAIN FAMILY FRUIT CAKE

8 oz (200 gm) self-raising flour
¼ level teaspoon salt
1 level teaspoon mixed spice
4 oz (100 gm) slightly softened
  butter, margarine or cooking fat
  (or mixture)
4 oz (100 gm) caster sugar
4 oz (100 gm) mixed dried fruit
1 standard egg, beaten
3 to 5 tablespoons cold milk

1. Pre-heat oven to moderate, 350°F
   or Gas No. 4 (177°C).
2. Brush inside of 6 inch (15 cm)
   round cake tin with melted white
   cooking fat. Line base and sides
   with greaseproof paper. Brush with
   more fat.
3. Sift flour, salt and spice into mixer
   bowl.
4. Cut butter, margarine or cooking fat
   (or mixture) into small pieces, and
   add to flour mixture.
5. With mixer at low speed, run
   beaters through ingredients until
   they resemble fine breadcrumbs.
6. Add sugar and dried fruit and,
   using fingertips, toss ingredients
   lightly together to mix.
7. With wooden spoon or fork, mix to
   medium stiff batter with beaten egg
   and milk, stirring briskly without
   beating.
8. Transfer to prepared tin.
9. Bake in centre of oven until well-
   risen and golden; 1¼ to 1½ hours,
   or until wooden cocktail stick,
   inserted into centre of cake, comes
   out clean.
10. Turn out and cool on wire rack.
11. Store in an air-tight tin when cold.

WALNUT, ORANGE, AND RAISIN LOAF

8 oz (200 gm) self-raising flour
¼ level teaspoon salt
4 oz (100 gm) slightly softened
  butter, margarine or cooking fat
  (or mixture)
4 oz (100 gm) caster sugar
1 oz (25 gm) shelled walnut
  halves, finely chopped*
3 oz (75 gm) seedless raisins
1 level teaspoon finely grated
  orange rind**
1 standard egg, beaten
3 to 5 tablespoons milk

1. Pre-heat oven to moderate, 350°F
   or Gas No. 4 (177°C).
2. Brush inside of 1 lb (approximately
   ½ kilo) loaf tin with melted white
   cooking fat. Line base and sides
   with greaseproof paper. Brush with
   more fat.
3. Sift flour and salt into mixer bowl.
4. Cut butter, margarine or cooking
   fat (or mixture) into small pieces
   and add to flour mixture.
5. With mixer at low speed, run
   beaters through ingredients until
   they resemble fine breadcrumbs.
6. Add sugar, walnuts, raisins, and
   orange rind. Using fingertips, toss
   ingredients lightly together to mix.
7. With wooden spoon or fork, mix
   to medium stiff batter with beaten
   egg and milk, stirring briskly without beating.
8. Transfer to prepared tin.
9. Bake in centre of oven until well-
   risen and golden; 1¼ to 1½ hours, or
   until wooden cocktail stick, inserted into centre of cake, comes
   out clean.
10. Turn out and cool on wire rack.
11. Store in an air-tight tin when cold.

Note

 *1. To chop nuts, put them, a few at a
     time, into blender. Run machine
     until finely chopped, but do not
     allow machine to over-run or nuts
     will become paste-like and oily.
**2. If preferred, put a long strip of
     orange rind into blender. Run
     machine until finely chopped.

CHERRY CAKE

3 oz (75 gm) glacé cherries
7 oz (175 gm) self-raising flour
¼ level teaspoon salt
1 oz (25 gm) semolina
**4 oz (100 gm) slightly softened
butter, margarine or cooking
fat (or mixture)**
4 oz (100 gm) caster sugar
**1 level teaspoon finely grated
lemon rind***
**1 teaspoon vanilla or almond
essence**
1 standard egg, beaten
5 tablespoons cold milk

1. Pre-heat oven to moderate, 350°F
   or Gas No. 4 (177°C).
2. Brush inside of 6 inch (15 cm)
   round cake tin with melted white
   cooking fat. Line base and sides
   with greaseproof paper. Brush
   paper with more fat.
3. Quarter cherries and wash
   thoroughly in warm water to remove syrup. Dry well in paper
   towels or tea towel. Put into bowl.
4. Sift flour, salt and semolina into
   mixer bowl.
5. Take out 2 tablespoonfuls, add to
   cherries, and toss with a metal
   spoon until pieces are well-
   coated.
6. Cut butter, margarine or cooking
   fat (or mixture) into small pieces,
   and add to flour and semolina
   mixture.
7. With mixer at low speed, run
   beaters through ingredients until
   they resemble fine breadcrumbs.
8. Add flour-coated cherry quarters,
   sugar, and lemon rind. Using
   fingertips, toss ingredients lightly
   together to mix.
9. With wooden spoon or fork, mix to
   medium stiff batter with essence,
   beaten egg and milk, stirring briskly
   without beating.
10. Transfer to prepared tin.
11. Bake in centre of oven until well-
    risen and golden; 1¼ to 1½ hours,
    or until wooden cocktail stick,
    inserted into centre of cake, comes
    out clean.
12. Turn out and cool on a wire rack.
13. Store in an air-tight tin when cold.

Note

*If preferred, put a long strip of lemon
 rind into blender. Run machine until
 rind is finely chopped.

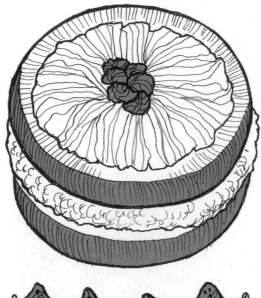

CHOCOLATE CHIP CAKE

8 oz (200 gm) self-raising flour
$\frac{1}{4}$ level teaspoon salt
4 oz (100 gm) slightly softened butter, margarine or cooking fat (or mixture)
4 oz (100 gm) caster sugar
4 oz (100 gm) chocolate drops or plain chocolate cut into small pieces
1 teaspoon vanilla essence
1 standard egg, beaten
3 to 5 tablespoons milk

1. Pre-heat oven to moderate, 350°F or Gas No. 4 (177°C).
2. Brush inside of 6 inch (15 cm) round cake tin with melted white cooking fat. Line base and sides with greaseproof paper. Brush paper with more fat.
3. Sift flour and salt into mixer bowl.
4. Cut butter, margarine or cooking fat (or mixture) into small pieces and add to flour.
5. With mixer at low speed, run beaters through ingredients until they resemble fine breadcrumbs.
6. Add sugar and chocolate and,

using fingertips, toss ingredients lightly together to mix.
7. With wooden spoon or fork, mix to a medium stiff batter with essence, beaten egg, and milk, stirring briskly without beating.
8. Transfer to prepared tin.
9. Bake in centre of oven until well-risen and golden; $1\frac{1}{4}$ to $1\frac{1}{2}$ hours, or until wooden cocktail stick, inserted into centre of cake, comes out clean.
10. Turn out and cool on a wire rack.
11. Store in an air-tight tin when cold.

CHOCOLATE BUNS

Makes 18 to 20

7 oz (175 gm) self-raising flour
1 oz (25 gm) cocoa powder
$\frac{1}{4}$ level teaspoon salt
4 oz (100 gm) slightly softened butter, margarine or cooking fat (or mixture)
4 oz (100 gm) caster or soft brown sugar
1 teaspoon vanilla essence
1 standard egg, beaten
3 to 5 tablespoons milk

1. Pre-heat oven to fairly hot, 375°F or Gas No. 5 (191°C).
2. Stand 18 to 20 paper cake cases in 18 to 20 ungreased bun tins, or alternatively brush 18 to 20 deep bun tins with melted white cooking fat.
3. Sift flour, cocoa and salt into mixer bowl.
4. Cut butter, margarine or cooking fat (or mixture) into small pieces, and add to flour and cocoa mixture.
5. With mixer at low speed, run beaters through ingredients until they resemble fine breadcrumbs.
6. Add sugar and, using fingertips, toss ingredients lightly together to mix.
7. With wooden spoon or fork, mix to medium stiff batter with essence, egg and milk, stirring briskly without beating.
8. Spoon equal amounts of mixture into cake cases or bun tins.
9. Bake just above centre of oven for 20 to 25 minutes, or until well-risen and golden.

70

10. Turn out and cool on a wire rack.
11. Store in an air-tight tin when cold.

ROCK BUNS

Makes 10

8 oz (200 gm) self-raising flour
¼ level teaspoon salt
3 oz (75 gm) slightly softened
  butter, margarine or cooking fat
  (or mixture)
3 oz (75 gm) caster sugar
2 oz (50 gm) currants
1 oz (25 gm) mixed chopped peel
1 level teaspoon finely grated
  lemon rind*
1 standard egg
2 to 3 dessertspoons cold milk

1. Pre-heat oven to fairly hot, 400°F
   or Gas No. 6 (200°C).
2. Sift flour and salt into mixer bowl.
3. Cut butter, margarine or cooking
   fat (or mixture) into small pieces,
   and add to flour mixture.
4. With mixer at low speed, run
   beaters through ingredients until
   they resemble fine breadcrumbs.
5. Add sugar, currants, chopped peel
   and lemon rind and, using fingertips, toss ingredients lightly together to mix.
6. Using a fork, mix to very stiff
   batter with beaten egg and milk.
7. Place 10 dessertspoons of mixture
   in rocky piles, on greased baking
   tray or trays, allowing room between each for them to spread.
8. Bake just above centre of oven 20
   to 25 minutes, or until well-risen
   and golden. Cool on a wire rack.
9. Store in an air-tight tin when cold.

Note

* If preferred, put a long strip of lemon
rind into blender. Run machine until
rind is finely chopped.

VICTORIA SANDWICH CAKE

4 oz (100 gm) self-raising flour
4 oz (100 gm) softened butter or
  margarine (or mixture)
4 oz (100 gm) caster sugar
1 teaspoon vanilla essence
  (optional)
2 standard eggs

Extra sugar for sprinkling over top
Jam for filling

1. Pre-heat oven to moderate, 350°F
   or Gas No. 4 (177°C).
2. Brush insides of two 7 inch
   (17.5 cm) sandwich tins with
   melted butter or white cooking fat.
   Line bases with rounds of greaseproof paper. Brush paper with more
   melted butter or fat.
3. Sift flour on to a plate.
4. Put butter or margarine with sugar
   and essence (if used) into mixer
   bowl. Cream with beaters until
   mixture is light and fluffy in texture.
5. Beat in whole eggs, one at a time,
   adding tablespoon of sifted flour
   with each.
6. Using metal spoon, gently fold in
   rest of flour.
7. Transfer to prepared tins, spreading
   mixture evenly with knife.
8. Bake in centre of oven for 20 to
   25 minutes, or until cakes are well-
   risen, golden brown, and have
   shrunk slightly away from sides of
   tins.
9. Turn out and cool on a wire rack.
   Remove paper.
10. When completely cold, sandwich
    together with jam and sprinkle top
    with caster sugar.

WALNUT SANDWICH CAKE

1. Follow recipe for Victoria Sandwich Cake, but stir 2 oz (50 gm)
   shelled walnuts, finely chopped,
   into mixture after beating in the
   eggs.
2. After cakes are cold, instead of
   using jam, sandwich them together with Coffee Butter Cream
   (page 81) and ice top with Coffee
   Glacé Icing (page 80). Alternatively, fill and coat top and sides
   with Seven Minute Frosting (page
   81).
3. Decorate top with extra shelled
   walnut halves.

Note

To chop nuts, put them, a few at a time,
into blender. Run machine until nuts
are fairly finely chopped, but do not
allow machine to over-run or nuts will
become paste-like and oily.

71

COFFEE SANDWICH CAKE

1. Follow recipe for Victoria Sandwich cake (page 71), but substitute 1 tablespoon very strong coffee or liquid coffee essence for vanilla essence.
2. Fold into mixture with flour.
3. When cakes are cold, instead of using jam, sandwich together with Coffee Butter Cream (page 81) and ice top with Coffee Glacé Icing (page 80).
4. Decorate with shelled walnut halves, toasted almonds, or hazelnuts.

ORANGE OR LEMON SANDWICH CAKE

1. Follow recipe for Victoria Sandwich Cake (page 71), but substitute finely grated orange or lemon rind for vanilla essence.
2. Cream grated rind with butter and sugar mixture.
3. When cakes are cold, instead of using jam, sandwich together with either orange or lemon Butter Cream (page 80) and ice top with Orange or Lemon Glacé Icing (page 80).
4. Decorate with pieces of orange or lemon slices (jellied type, coated with sugar, and available from sweet shops) or with pieces of angelica.

CHOCOLATE SANDWICH CAKE

4 oz (100 gm) self-raising flour
2 tablespoons boiling water
2 level tablespoons cocoa powder
4 oz (100 gm) softened butter or margarine (or mixture)
5 oz (125 gm) soft brown sugar
1 teaspoon vanilla essence
2 standard eggs
1 tablespoon milk

1. Pre-heat oven to moderate, 350°F or Gas No. 4 (177°C).
2. Brush insides of two 7 inch (17.5 cm) sandwich tins with melted butter or white cooking fat. Line bases with rounds of greaseproof paper. Brush paper with more melted butter or fat.

3. Sift flour thoroughly on to a plate.
4. Gradually add boiling water to cocoa, and stir until smooth. Leave to cool.
5. Put butter or margarine with sugar and essence into mixer bowl. Cream with beaters until mixture is light and fluffy in texture.
6. Gradually beat in cooled cocoa mixture.
7. Beat in whole eggs, one at a time, adding tablespoon of sifted flour mixture with each.
8. Stir in milk, then, using metal spoon, gently fold in rest of flour.
9. Transfer to prepared tins, spreading mixture evenly with a knife.
10. Bake in centre of oven for 20 to 25 minutes, or until cakes are firm and well-risen, and have shrunk slightly away from sides of tin.
11. Turn out and cool on a wire rack. Remove paper.
12. When completely cold, sandwich together with Basic Butter Cream (page 80) and ice top with Chocolate Glacé Icing (page 80). Alternatively, sandwich cakes together and cover top with slightly sweetened whipped cream.
13. Decorate with grated chocolate, halved glacé cherries, or flaked and toasted almonds.

FAIRY CAKES

Makes 18 to 20

4 oz (100 gm) self-raising flour
4 oz (100 gm) softened butter or margarine (or mixture)
4 oz (100 gm) caster sugar
1 teaspoon finely grated lemon rind*
2 standard eggs
1½ oz (37 gm) currants
1½ oz (37 gm) glacé cherries, finely chopped

1. Pre-heat oven to fairly hot, 375°F or Gas No. 5 (191°C).
2. Stand 18 to 20 paper cake cases in 18 to 20 ungreased bun tins, or alternatively brush 18 to 20 deep bun tins with melted white cooking fat.
3. Sift flour on to a plate.
4. Put butter or margarine with sugar

and lemon rind into mixer bowl.
Cream with beaters until mixture
is light and fluffy in texture.

5. Beat in whole eggs, one at a time,
   adding tablespoon of sifted flour
   with each.
6. Stir in currants and cherries.
7. Using metal spoon, gently fold in
   rest of flour.
8. Spoon equal amounts of mixture
   into cake cases or bun tins.
9. Bake in centre of oven for 20 to
   25 minutes, or until cakes are well-
   risen and golden.
10. Turn out and cool on a wire rack.
11. Store in an air-tight tin when cold.

Note

* If preferred, put a long strip of lemon
rind into blender. Run machine until
rind is finely chopped.

MADELEINES

Makes 12

4 oz (100 gm) self-raising flour
4 oz (100 gm) softened butter or
margarine (or mixture)
4 oz (100 gm) caster sugar
2 standard eggs
Apricot jam
Desiccated coconut
6 glacé cherries, halved
2 dozen small leaves, cut from
angelica

1. Pre-heat oven to moderate, 350°F
   or Gas No. 4 (177°C).
2. Sift flour on to plate.
3. Put butter or margarine with caster
   sugar into mixer bowl. Cream with
   beaters until mixture is light and
   fluffy in texture.
4. Beat in whole eggs, one at a time,
   adding tablespoon of sifted flour
   with each.
5. Using metal spoon, gently fold in
   rest of flour.
6. Spoon equal amounts of mixture
   into 12 greased dariole moulds
   (castle pudding tins).
7. Stand on baking tray and bake in
   centre of oven for 20 to 25
   minutes, or until well-risen and
   golden.
8. Turn out and cool on a wire rack.
9. When completely cold, cut a thin

slice from the wide end of each
Madeleine, so that it can stand
upright without toppling.
10. Brush Madeleines all over with
    warm apricot jam, then roll each
    in coconut. Stand half a cherry and
    2 leaves of angelica on the top of
    each.

DUNDEE CAKE

8 oz (100 gm) plain flour
2 level teaspoons mixed spice
Pinch of salt
8 oz (200 gm) softened butter or
  margarine (or mixture)
8 oz (200 gm) soft brown sugar
1 level teaspoon finely grated
  orange rind*
4 standard eggs
2 oz (50 gm) whole almonds,
  blanched and finely chopped**
1 lb ($\frac{1}{2}$ kilo) mixed dried fruit
2 oz (50 gm) mixed chopped peel
2 oz (50 gm) glacé cherries

TOPPING

2 oz (50 gm) whole almonds,
  blanched and split

1. Pre-heat oven to cool, 300°F or
   Gas No. 2 (149°C).
2. Brush inside of 7 inch (17.5 cm)
   round cake tin with melted butter
   or white cooking fat. Line base and
   sides with greaseproof paper. Brush
   paper with more butter or fat.
3. Sift flour, spice, and salt on to a
   plate.
4. Put butter or margarine with sugar
   and orange rind into mixer bowl.
   Cream with beaters until light and
   fluffy in texture.
5. Beat in whole eggs, one at a time,
   adding tablespoon of sifted dry
   ingredients with each.
6. Stir in chopped almonds, fruit,
   peel, and cherries.
7. Using metal spoon, gently fold in
   rest of flour.
8. Transfer to prepared tin, spreading
   mixture evenly with a knife.
9. Arrange split almonds, in circles,
   on top.
10. Put into centre of oven and bake
    $3\frac{1}{2}$ to $4\frac{1}{4}$ hours, until well-risen and

golden, or until wooden cocktail
stick, inserted into centre of cake,
comes out clean.
11. Leave in tin 15 minutes, then turn
    out and cool on wire rack.
12. Store in an air-tight tin when cold.

Note

1. To protect the sides of the cake
   from scorching, it is advisable to
   tie a strip of brown paper, folded
   double, to the outside of the tin.
2. If the top of the cake seems to be
   over-browning, cover with a
   double thickness of damp greaseproof paper about halfway
   through cooking time.
*3. If preferred, put long strip of
   orange rind into blender. Run
   machine until rind is finely
   chopped.
**4. To chop nuts put them, a few at
   a time, into blender. Run machine
   until nuts are fairly finely chopped,
   but do not allow machine to over-
   run or nuts will become paste-
   like and oily.

PLAIN MADEIRA CAKE

8 oz (200 gm) plain flour
2 level teaspoons baking powder
Pinch of salt
6 oz (150 gm) softened butter or
  margarine (or mixture)
6 oz (150 gm) caster sugar
Finely grated rind of 1 lemon*
1 teaspoon vanilla essence
3 standard eggs
2 tablespoons milk
2 strips crystallized citron peel
  (optional)

1. Pre-heat oven to warm, 325°F or
   Gas No. 3 (173°C).
2. Brush inside of 6 inch (15 cm)
   round cake tin or 1 lb (approxi-

mately ½ kilo) loaf tin with melted butter or white cooking fat. Line base and sides with greaseproof paper. Brush paper with more fat.

3. Sift flour, baking powder and salt on to a plate.

4. Put butter or margarine with sugar, lemon rind, and essence into mixer bowl. Cream with beaters until mixture is light and fluffy in texture.

5. Beat in whole eggs, one at a time, adding tablespoon of sifted flour with each.

6. Using metal spoon, gently fold in rest of flour alternately with milk.

7. Transfer to prepared tin, spreading mixture evenly with a knife. Place strips of citron peel, if used, on top of cake mixture.

8. Bake in centre of oven for 1½ to 1¾ hours until well-risen and golden, or until wooden cocktail stick, inserted into centre of cake, comes out clean.

9. Leave in tin 5 minutes, then turn out and cool on wire rack.

10. Store in air-tight tin when cold.

Note

* If preferred, peel lemon and put rind into blender. Run machine until rind is finely chopped.

CHRISTMAS CAKE

8 oz (200 gm) plain flour
1 oz (25 gm) cocoa powder
2 level teaspoons mixed spice
1 level teaspoon cinnamon
Pinch of salt
8 oz (200 gm) softened butter or margarine (or mixture)
8 oz (200 gm) soft brown sugar
1 level teaspoon *each*, grated orange and lemon rind*
4 standard eggs
8 oz (200 gm) *each*, sultanas, currants and seedless raisins
4 oz (100 gm) mixed chopped peel
4 oz (100 gm) dates, fairly finely chopped
2 oz (50 gm) glacé cherries, chopped
2 oz (50 gm) shelled walnut halves, chopped**
2 oz (50 gm) whole almonds, blanched and chopped**
1 tablespoon black treacle

1. Pre-heat oven to very cool, 275°F or Gas No. 1 (135°C).

2. Brush inside of 8 inch (20 cm) round cake tin or 7 inch (17.5 cm) square cake tin with melted butter or white cooking fat. Line base and sides with double thickness of greaseproof paper. Brush paper with more butter or fat.

3. Tie strip of brown paper, folded double, round outside of tin to prevent sides of cake from scorching.

4. Sift flour, cocoa powder, spice, cinnamon and salt on to a plate.

5. Put butter or margarine with sugar, and orange and lemon rind into mixer bowl. Cream with beaters until light and fluffy in texture.

6. Beat in whole eggs, one at a time, adding tablespoon of sifted dry ingredients with each.

7. Using metal spoon, gently stir in *half* the dried fruit, chopped peel, dates, cherries, nuts, and dry ingredients. When well blended, stir in all remaining ingredients plus treacle.

8. Transfer to prepared tin, spreading mixture evenly with a knife.

9. Put into centre of oven and bake for 4½ to 5 hours, or until wooden cocktail stick, inserted into centre of cake, comes out clean.

10. Leave in tin 30 minutes, then carefully turn out on to wire rack.

11. When completely cold, wrap in foil and store in an air-tight tin for between 1 and 4 weeks, so that cake has time to mature.

12. Coat top only, or both top and sides, with Almond Paste (page 80). Wrap and leave at least 24 hours. Afterwards coat with Royal Icing (page 81) and decorate with Christmas Cake novelties.

Note

*1. If preferred, put a long strip of both orange and lemon rind into blender. Run machine until rind is finely chopped.

**2. To chop nuts put them, a few at a time, into blender. Run machine until nuts are fairly finely chopped, but do not allow machine to over-run or nuts will become paste-like and oily.

VIENNA WHIRLS

Makes 12

7 oz (175 gm) plain flour
1 oz (25 gm) cornflour
Pinch of salt
8 oz (200 gm) softened butter or
  margarine
3 oz (75 gm) icing sugar, sifted
1 teaspoon vanilla essence
Extra icing sugar and red jam for
  decoration

1. Pre-heat oven to moderate, 350°F or Gas No. 4 (177°C).
2. Stand 12 paper cake cases in 12 ungreased bun tins.
3. Sift flour, cornflour and salt into bowl.
4. Put butter or margarine with sugar and essence into mixer bowl. Cream with beaters until mixture is light and fluffy in texture.
5. Using metal spoon, gently stir in flour mixture.
6. When mixture is smooth and well-blended, transfer to forcing bag with ½ inch star-shaped icing pipe.
7. Pipe whirls of mixture into paper cake cases, leaving a small hollow in centre of each.
8. Bake in centre of oven for 20 to 25 minutes, or until just golden.
9. Cool on a wire rack, then dust tops of whirls lightly with sifted icing sugar.
10. Put a small blob of jam in the centre of each.

BLACKBERRY CRACKLE CAKE

8 oz (200 gm) self-raising flour
Pinch of salt
2 oz (50 gm) softened butter or
  margarine
4 oz (100 gm) caster sugar
1 teaspoon vanilla essence
1 large egg
¼ pint (125 ml) cold milk
4 oz (100 gm) fresh blackberries,
  washed and well-drained
1 level teaspoon cinnamon
1 level tablespoon extra caster
  sugar

1. Pre-heat oven to fairly hot, 375°F or Gas No. 5 (191°C).

2. Brush inside of 8 inch (20 cm) sandwich tin with melted butter or white cooking fat. Line base with round of greaseproof paper. Brush paper with more butter or fat.
3. Sift flour and salt on to a plate.
4. Put butter or margarine with sugar and essence into mixer bowl. Cream with beaters until light and fluffy in texture.
5. Add whole egg and then, with mixer at low speed, gradually add sifted flour alternately with the milk. Beat for ½ minute.
6. Transfer mixture to prepared tin, then cover top with blackberries.
7. Mix together cinnamon and sugar, and sprinkle over fruit.
8. Bake in centre of oven for 45 minutes to 1 hour, or until wooden cocktail stick, inserted into centre of cake, comes out clean.
9. Cool to lukewarm in the tin, then cut into wedges.
10. Bake and eat on same day.

FRUIT AND CREAM SPONGE GATEAU

3 oz (75 gm) plain flour
Pinch of salt
3 standard eggs
3 oz (75 gm) caster sugar
½ pint (250 ml) double cream
2 tablespoons cold milk
3 tablespoons sifted icing sugar
Fresh or canned fruit to taste*
Melted and strained apricot jam

1. Pre-heat oven to moderate, 350°F or Gas No. 4 (177°C).
2. Brush inside of 7 inch (17.5 cm) round cake tin with melted butter or margarine. Line base and sides with greaseproof paper. Brush paper with more butter or fat.
3. Sift flour and salt twice on to a plate.
4. Break eggs into mixer bowl. Add sugar.
5. Beat with beaters for 5 to 7 minutes, until mixture is very pale in colour, the consistency of softly whipped cream, and at least twice its original volume.
6. Very gradually add flour, gently and lightly cutting it through the

mixture with a metal spoon.

7. Transfer to prepared tin, spreading mixture evenly with a knife.
8. Bake in centre of oven for 45 minutes to 1 hour, or until top of cake springs back when pressed lightly with the finger.
9. Turn out on to sheet of sugared greaseproof paper standing on damp tea towel. Remove greaseproof lining paper. Leave cake until completely cold.
10. Put cream, milk, and icing sugar into clean mixer bowl. With mixer at low speed, beat with beaters until stiff.
11. Cut cake into 3 layers and sandwich together generously with cream.
12. Spread more cream over the top, then cover with fresh or canned fruit.
13. Glaze fruit by brushing with jam.
14. With remaining cream, pipe rosettes or whirls round top edge of cake, using a pipe and forcing bag.
15. Make and eat Gateau on same day.

Note

* For fresh fruit, use halved and de-seeded grapes, raspberries, halved strawberries, or loganberries. For canned fruit, use well-drained peaches, apricot halves, pineapple pieces, pear halves, or gooseberries.

MERINGUES

Makes 8

2 egg whites
Pinch of cream of tartar
5 oz (125 gm) caster sugar
2 level teaspoons cornflour
¼ pint (125 ml) double cream
1 tablespoon milk

1. Pre-heat oven to very cool, 225°F or Gas No. ¼ (107°C).
2. Brush large baking tray or two smaller ones with salad oil. Cover base, or bases, with double thickness of greaseproof paper. Leave paper ungreased.
3. Put egg whites into clean, dry mixer bowl. Add cream of tartar.
4. Beat with beaters until whites are stiff and snow-like.
5. Add half the sugar. Continue

beating until meringue is very shiny and stands in stiff, firm peaks.
6. With metal spoon, gently fold in remaining sugar, and cornflour.
7. Using dessertspoon, place 16 ovals on prepared tray or trays or, if preferred, pipe meringues in rounds using a large star-shaped tube and forcing bag.
8. Put into centre of oven and bake for 1½ hours.
9. Remove from oven and peel carefully away from paper.
10. Using thumb, gently press a small hollow in the base of each meringue.
11. Stand upside down (with hollows facing upwards) on baking tray, and bake for a further 45 minutes.
12. Transfer to wire rack and leave until completely cold.
13. Put cream and milk into mixer bowl. With mixer at low speed, beat with beaters until stiff. Sandwich meringues together, in pairs, with whipped cream.

Note

Meringues, provided they are well dried out, can be stored in an air-tight tin almost indefinitely. However, once they are cream-filled, they should be eaten on the same day.

CHOCOLATE ECLAIRS

Makes 12

2½ oz (62 gm) plain flour
Pinch of salt
¼ pint (125 ml) water
2 oz (50 gm) butter or margarine
2 standard eggs, lightly beaten

1. Pre-heat oven to fairly hot, 400°F or Gas No. 6 (204°C).
2. Place plain ½ inch icing pipe in forcing bag.
3. Sift flour and salt twice on to a plate.
4. Put water, and butter or margarine into saucepan. Heat gently until butter or margarine melts, then bring to a brisk boil.
5. Remove from heat and tip in the flour all at once. Return to very low heat.
6. Beat with a wooden spoon until mixture forms a ball in the middle of the pan, leaving sides of pan clean. Cool slightly.
7. With portable or hand-held mixer running at low speed, beat in eggs very gradually.
8. Beat until mixture is smooth, shiny and sufficiently firm to stand in soft peaks.
9. Transfer to forcing bag and pipe approximately 12 lengths, each 3 to 4 inches (7.5 to 10 cm) long, on greased baking tray.
10. Bake towards top of oven for 20 minutes. Reduce oven temperature to moderate, 350°F or Gas No. 4 (177°C), and bake a further 20 to 25 minutes, or until Eclairs are well-puffed and golden.
11. Remove from oven, and with sharp knife make a slit along the side of each to allow steam to escape. Cool on a wire rack.
12. When completely cool, fill with sweetened whipped cream.
13. Coat the tops with Chocolate Glacé Icing (page 80).
14. Make and eat on same day.

COFFEE CREAM BUNS

1. Follow recipe for Chocolate Eclairs, but pipe 12 rounds on greased baking trays.
2. Cover trays with roasting tins, or buns will collapse, and bake in centre of oven for 45 to 50 minutes.
3. Continue as for Chocolate Eclairs, but ice tops by dipping in Coffee Glacé Icing (page 80).

SACHERTORTE

An Austrian speciality

3 oz (75 gm) plain chocolate
1 tablespoon very strong coffee
1 teaspoon vanilla essence
2½ oz (62 gm) plain flour
2½ oz (62 gm) softened butter or margarine
2½ oz (62 gm) icing sugar, sifted
3 large eggs, separated
Apricot jam

1. Pre-heat oven to moderate, 350°F or Gas No. 4 (177°C).
2. Brush 7 inch (17.5 cm) loose-bottomed round cake tin with melted butter. Line base and sides with greaseproof paper. Brush paper with more butter.
3. Break up chocolate and put into basin with coffee and essence. Leave over a saucepan of hot, but not boiling, water until melted, stirring once or twice. Leave to cool.
4. Sift flour twice on to a plate.
5. Put butter or margarine with 1½ oz (37 gm) sugar into mixer bowl. Cream with beaters until light and fluffy in texture.
6. Beat in egg yolks and cooled chocolate mixture. Transfer to second bowl.
7. Put egg whites in clean, dry mixer bowl and beat to a stiff snow. Add remaining sugar. Continue beating until whites are shiny and stand in high, firm peaks.
8. Using a metal spoon, gently fold into chocolate mixture alternately with flour.
9. When smoothly mixed, transfer to prepared tin.
10. Bake in centre of oven for 40 to 50 minutes, or until wooden cocktail stick, inserted into centre of cake, comes out clean.
11. Leave in tin 5 minutes, then turn

out and cool on a wire rack. Remove paper.

12. When cake is completely cold, cut in half and sandwich together with apricot jam. Warm some more apricot jam, and brush over top and sides of cake to hold crumbs in place and prevent them mingling with the icing.

13. Stand cake on rack and cover top and sides with Mocha Icing (page 80).

14. When serving cake accompany, in traditional style, with a bowl of softly whipped cream.

DEVIL'S FOOD CAKE

7 oz (175 gm) self-raising flour
2 oz (50 gm) cocoa powder
1 level teaspoon bicarbonate of soda
$\frac{1}{4}$ pint (125 ml) warm water
4 tablespoons salad oil

2 large eggs
1 teaspoon vanilla essence
8 oz (200 gm) golden syrup, warmed until liquid

1. Pre-heat oven to warm, 325°F or Gas No. 3 (163°C).
2. Brush oblong tin, measuring approximately 7 inches by 9 inches by 2 inches deep (17.5 cm by 22.5 cm by 5 cm), with melted butter or margarine. Line base and sides with greaseproof paper. Brush paper with more butter or margarine.
3. Sift flour, cocoa and bicarbonate of soda into bowl.
4. Put water, oil, eggs, essence and syrup into mixer bowl. With mixer at low speed, beat with beaters for 1 minute.
5. Gradually add dry ingredients and beat at medium speed for a further 7 minutes.
6. Transfer to prepared tin.
7. Bake in centre of oven for 1 hour, or until wooden cocktail stick, inserted into centre of cake, comes out clean.
8. Leave in tin 5 minutes, then turn out and cool on a wire rack. Remove paper.
9. When cake is completely cold, cut in half and sandwich together with whipped cream or Basic Butter Cream (page 80). Coat top and sides with Seven Minute Frosting (page 81).

Cake Icings & Fillings

BASIC GLACÉ ICING

4 oz (100 gm) icing sugar, sifted
3 to 4 teaspoons warm water

1. Put icing sugar into mixer bowl. With mixer at low speed, gradually beat in water, and continue beating for about $\frac{1}{4}$ minute, or until quite smooth.
2. If liked, colour pale pink, yellow, orange, green, or blue by stirring in the appropriate colourings.
3. Use straight away.

Note

1. If icing is too thin, add a little sifted icing sugar. If too thick, beat in a little more warm water.
2. The above quantity is sufficient to cover top of 7 inch (17.5 cm) cake. To coat the sides as well, make up double quantity of icing.

79

ORANGE OR LEMON GLACÉ ICING

Follow recipe for Basic Glacé Icing, but substitute strained orange or lemon juice for warm water and add appropriate food colouring.

COFFEE GLACÉ ICING

Follow recipe for Basic Glacé Icing, but dissolve 1 or 2 teaspoons instant coffee granules in 3 teaspoons of hot water and use instead of warm water.

CHOCOLATE GLACÉ ICING

2 oz (50 gm) plain chocolate
1 teaspoon butter
½ teaspoon vanilla essence
2 tablespoons warm water
4 oz (100 gm) icing sugar, sifted

1. Break up chocolate and put into basin with butter, essence, and water.
2. Stand basin over pan of hot, but not boiling, water.
3. Leave until melted, stirring once or twice.
4. Put icing sugar into mixer bowl. With mixer at low speed, gradually beat in chocolate mixture, and continue beating for about ¼ minute, or until icing is smooth.
5. Use straight away.

MOCHA ICING

4 oz (100 gm) plain chocolate
1 teaspoon butter
2 teaspoons instant coffee granules or powder
8 teaspoons hot water
2 oz (50 gm) icing sugar, sifted

1. Break up chocolate and put into basin with butter, coffee and 3 teaspoons hot water.
2. Stand basin over saucepan of hot, but not boiling, water. Leave until melted, stirring once or twice.
3. Put icing sugar into mixer bowl. With mixer at low speed, gradually beat in chocolate mixture alternately with remaining water, and continue beating for about ¼ minute, or until icing is smooth.
4. Use straight away.

ALMOND PASTE

1 large egg + 1 yolk
1 teaspoon lemon juice
½ teaspoon vanilla essence
½ teaspoon almond essence
12 oz (300 gm) ground almonds
6 oz (150 gm) icing sugar, sifted
6 oz (150 gm) caster sugar

1. Put egg, yolk, lemon juice, and essences into mixer bowl.
2. With mixer at low speed, beat with beaters until well blended.
3. Put all remaining ingredients into second bowl.
4. Using a fork, work to a stiff paste with egg mixture.
5. Turn out on to a surface dusted with sifted icing sugar, and knead until smooth.

Note

1. This quantity of Almond Paste is sufficient to cover the top and sides of a 7 to 8 inch (17.5 to 20 cm) rich fruit cake.
2. If Almond Paste is too soft, work in a little extra sifted icing sugar. If too stiff, add a little more beaten egg or lemon juice.

BASIC BUTTER CREAM

4 oz (100 gm) softened butter
1 teaspoon vanilla essence
8 oz (200 gm) icing sugar, sifted
2 tablespoons milk or single cream

1. Rinse mixer bowl with hot water and wipe dry.
2. Add butter and vanilla.
3. With mixer at low speed, cream butter with beaters until very soft.
4. Gradually beat in icing sugar alternately with milk or cream.
5. With mixer at medium speed, continue beating until mixture is light and fluffy.

Note

1. If liked, colour Butter Cream pale pink, yellow, orange, or green by beating in the appropriate food colouring.
2. To flavour Butter Cream orange or lemon, add 1 teaspoon grated

orange or lemon rind when beating in the icing sugar.

3. The above quantity is sufficient to fill and cover top and sides of a 7 inch (17.5 cm) sandwich cake. If Butter Cream is wanted only for the top, sides, or as a filling, make up half quantity.

COFFEE BUTTER CREAM

4 rounded teaspoons instant coffee granules or powder
1 dessertspoon boiling water
4 oz (100 gm) softened butter
8 oz (200 gm) icing sugar, sifted
1 tablespoon milk or single cream

1. Dissolve coffee in the boiling water and leave to cool.
2. Rinse mixer bowl with hot water and wipe dry.
3. Add butter. With mixer at low speed, cream butter with beaters until very soft.
4. Gradually beat in sugar alternately with dissolved coffee, and milk or cream.
5. With mixer at medium speed, continue beating until mixture is light and fluffy.

ROYAL ICING

3 egg whites
1½ lb (approximately ¾ kilo) icing sugar, sifted
¼ teaspoon glycerine

1. With mixer at medium speed, beat egg whites with beaters until foamy.
2. With mixer at low speed, gradually beat in icing sugar.
3. When all the icing sugar has been incorporated, add glycerine (which makes icing less brittle).
4. Continue beating at medium speed for about 7 minutes, or until icing is very smooth and white, and forms soft peaks.
5. Cover with a damp tea towel or sheet of damp greaseproof paper, and leave to stand for 1 hour.
6. Before using, add 1 tablespoon hot water, and stir icing gently with a wooden spoon to break up any bubbles that may have formed while it was being beaten.

Note

1. The above quantity will twice coat top and sides of a 7 to 8 inch (17.5 to 20 cm) rich fruit cake.
2. For 'rough' icing used to cover a Christmas cake, reduce quantity of icing sugar by about 4 oz (100 gm), and beat until icing forms peaks.
3. When icing is being used for piping, make the same consistency as above, but omit glycerine.

SEVEN MINUTE FROSTING

1 egg white
6 oz (150 gm) granulated sugar
2 tablespoons boiling water
1 teaspoon vanilla essence
¼ level teaspoon cream of tartar

1. Put all ingredients into large basin.
2. Stand basin over saucepan of hot water.
3. With portable or hand-held mixer running at high speed, beat frosting with beaters for approximately 7 minutes, or until it thickens sufficiently to form peaks.
4. Spread over cake straight away and leave until set.

Note

1. To make orange or lemon frosting, add a few drops of orange or lemon essence to the ingredients before beating the mixture. Colour pale orange or yellow with food colouring.
2. To make coffee frosting, dissolve 1 or 2 teaspoons instant coffee granules or powder in the boiling water.

Basic Yeast Cookery

SIMPLE WHITE BREAD

1 level teaspoon sugar
½ pint (250 ml) warm water
2 level teaspoons dried yeast
1 lb (approximately ½ kilo) plain
   flour
2 level teaspoons salt
A little milk for brushing

1. Pre-heat oven to very hot, 450°F or Gas No. 8 (232°C).
2. Dissolve sugar in half the water. Sprinkle yeast on top. Leave to stand in a warm place for 10 to 15 minutes, or until frothy.
3. Sift flour and salt into mixer bowl. Add yeast liquid with remaining warm water.
4. Mix to a dough with dough hook, then continue to knead with hook until dough is smooth and elastic.
5. Cover with a piece of greased polythene and leave to rise in a warm place for about 1 hour, or until dough has doubled in size and springs back when pressed lightly with the finger.
6. Uncover and knead dough lightly with hook until firm.
7. Put into greased 2 lb (approximately 1 kilo) loaf tin and cover with greased polythene.
8. Leave in a warm place until dough has again doubled in size and reaches top of tin.
9. Brush with milk and bake in centre of oven for 30 to 40 minutes, or until loaf has shrunk away slightly from sides of tin, and crust is golden brown.
10. Turn out and cool on a wire rack.

QUICK WHOLEMEAL BREAD

1 level teaspoon sugar
½ pint (250 ml) warm water
2 level teaspoons dried yeast
8 oz (200 gm) wholemeal flour
8 oz (200 gm) plain flour
2 level teaspoons salt

1 oz (25 gm) lard or cooking fat
Milk for brushing

1. Pre-heat oven to very hot, 450°F or Gas No. 8 (232°C).
2. Dissolve sugar in half the warm water. Sprinkle yeast on top. Leave to stand in a warm place for 10 to 15 minutes, or until frothy.
3. Sift flours and salt into mixer bowl. Rub in lard or cooking fat finely.
4. Add yeast liquid with remaining warm water.
5. Mix to a dough with dough hook, then continue to knead with hook until dough is smooth and elastic.
6. Divide dough in two and put into two greased 1 lb (approximately ½ kilo) loaf tins.
7. Cover with polythene, and leave to rise until dough has doubled in size and reaches tops of tins.
8. Brush with milk and bake in centre of oven for 30 to 40 minutes, or until loaves have shrunk away slightly from sides of tins, and crust is golden brown.
9. Turn out and cool on a wire rack.

WHOLEMEAL ROLLS

Makes 12

1. Follow recipe for Wholemeal Bread.
2. After kneading, divide dough into 12 equal portions.
3. Shape into round rolls.
4. Stand about 1 inch apart on greased and floured baking tray. Cover and leave to rise until double in size.
5. Brush tops with milk and bake towards top of very hot oven, 450°F or Gas No. 8 (232°C), for 20 to 25 minutes.
6. Cool on a wire rack.

FRUIT BREAD

4 level teaspoons caster sugar
¼ pint (125 ml) warm water
1 level tablespoon dried yeast

1 lb (approximately ½ kilo) plain
  flour
1 level teaspoon salt
1 oz (25 gm) margarine or cooking
  fat
2 oz (50 gm) currants
2 oz (50 gm) sultanas
2 oz (50 gm) mixed chopped peel
¼ pint (125 ml) warm milk

GLAZE

1 level tablespoon granulated
  sugar
1 tablespoon milk

1. Pre-heat oven to hot, 425°F or
   Gas No. 7 (218°C).
2. Dissolve 1 teaspoon sugar in the
   warm water. Sprinkle yeast on top.
   Leave to stand in a warm place for
   10 to 15 minutes, or until frothy.
3. Sift flour and salt into mixer bowl.
4. Rub in margarine or fat finely.
5. Add rest of sugar, fruit, and peel.
6. Add yeast liquid and warm milk.
7. Mix to a dough with dough hook,
   then continue to knead with hook
   until dough is smooth and elastic.
8. Cover with a piece of greased
   polythene and leave to rise in a
   warm place for about 1 hour, or
   until dough has doubled in size and
   springs back when pressed lightly
   with the finger.
9. Uncover and knead lightly with the
   hook until firm.
10. Put into greased 2 lb (approxim-
    ately 1 kilo) loaf tin and cover with
    greased polythene.
11. Leave in a warm place until dough
    has again doubled in size, and
    reaches top of tin.
12. Bake in centre of oven for 45
    minutes, or until loaf has shrunk
    away slightly from sides of tin, and
    crust is golden brown.
13. Remove from tin and transfer to
    wire cooling rack.
14. Make glaze, by dissolving sugar in
    the milk and boiling for 1 minute.
    Brush over top of loaf.

HOT CROSS BUNS
Makes 12

2 oz (50 gm) caster sugar

¼ pint (125 ml) warm water
1 level tablespoon dried yeast
1 lb (approximately ½ kilo) plain
  flour
1 level teaspoon salt
1 level teaspoon mixed spice
1 level teaspoon cinnamon
¼ level teaspoon cloves
2 oz (50 gm) butter or margarine
4 oz (100 gm) currants
2 oz (50 gm) mixed chopped peel
5 tablespoons warm milk
1 standard egg, fork-beaten

GLAZE

2 level tablespoons granulated
  sugar
2 tablespoons milk

1. Pre-heat oven to hot, 425°F or
   Gas No. 7 (218°C).
2. Dissolve 2 teaspoons of the sugar
   in the water. Sprinkle yeast on top.
   Leave to stand in a warm place for
   10 to 15 minutes, or until frothy.
3. Sift flour, salt and spices into mixer
   bowl.
4. Rub in butter or margarine, then
   add rest of sugar, currants and peel.
   Toss ingredients lightly together.
5. Add yeast liquid, milk and egg.
6. Mix to a dough with dough hook,
   then continue to knead with hook
   until dough is smooth and elastic.
7. Cover with a piece of greased
   polythene and leave to rise in a
   warm place for about 1 hour, or
   until dough has doubled in size and
   springs back when pressed lightly
   with the finger.
8. Uncover and knead lightly with
   hook until firm.
9. Divide into 12 equal-sized pieces
   and shape each into a round bun.
10. Stand on greased baking trays and
    cover with greased polythene.
11. Leave to rise again in a warm place
    until double in size.
12. Cut a cross on the top of each with
    a knife.
13. Bake just above centre of oven for
    20 to 25 minutes.
14. Remove from oven.
15. Make glaze, by dissolving sugar in
    the milk and boiling for 1 minute.
    Brush over tops of buns.
16. Cool on a wire rack.

DEVONSHIRE SPLITS

Makes 14

2 oz (50 gm) caster sugar
¼ pint (125 ml) water
1 level tablespoon dried yeast
1 lb (approximately ½ kilo) plain flour
1 level teaspoon salt
2 oz (50 gm) butter or margarine, melted
¼ pint (125 ml) warm milk

FILLING

Red jam
Clotted or whipped cream

1. Pre-heat oven to hot, 425°F or Gas No. 7 (218°C).
2. Dissolve 2 teaspoons sugar in the water. Sprinkle yeast on top. Leave to stand in a warm place for 10 to 15 minutes, or until frothy.
3. Sift flour and salt into mixer bowl. Add rest of sugar.
4. Add yeast liquid with melted butter or margarine, and milk.
5. Mix to dough with dough hook, then continue to knead with hook until dough is smooth and elastic.
6. Cover with greased polythene and leave to rise in a warm place for about 1 hour, or until dough has doubled in size and springs back when pressed lightly with the finger.
7. Uncover and knead lightly with hook until firm.
8. Divide into 14 equal-sized pieces and shape each into round bun.
9. Stand on greased baking tray and cover with greased polythene.
10. Leave to rise again in a warm place, until double in size.
11. Bake just above centre of oven for 20 to 25 minutes.
12. Transfer to wire cooling rack.
13. When completely cold, cut each in half and fill with jam and cream.
14. Dust tops with sifted icing sugar.

CHELSEA BUNS

Makes 12

3 oz (75 gm) caster sugar
¼ pint (125 ml) warm water
1 level tablespoon dried yeast

1 lb. (approximately ½ kilo) plain flour
1 level teaspoon salt
3 oz (75 gm) butter or margarine
¼ pint (125 ml) warm milk
6 oz (150 gm) currants

1. Pre-heat oven to hot, 425°F or Gas No. 7 (218°C).
2. Dissolve 2 teaspoons sugar in the water. Sprinkle yeast on top. Leave to stand in a warm place for 10 to 15 minutes, or until frothy.
3. Sift flour and salt into bowl. Rub in half the butter or margarine finely.
4. Add yeast liquid with warm milk.
5. Mix to dough with dough hook, then continue to knead with hook until dough is smooth and elastic.
6. Cover with greased polythene and leave to rise in a warm place for about 1 hour, or until dough has doubled in size and springs back when pressed lightly with the finger.
7. Uncover and knead lightly with hook until firm.
8. Turn on to floured surface and roll into a rectangle measuring 14 inches by 10 inches (35 cm by 25 cm).
9. Melt remaining butter. Brush over dough to within ½ inch of edges.
10. Sprinkle with rest of sugar and currants, then roll up like a Swiss roll, starting from one of the longer sides.
11. Cut into 12 slices and stand on greased baking tray, cut sides uppermost.
12. Cover with greased polythene and leave to rise again in a warm place, until double in size.
13. Bake just above centre of oven for 20 to 25 minutes.
14. Transfer to wire cooling rack.
15. When completely cold, cover tops of each with Glacé Icing (page 79).

RUM BABAS

Makes 12

1 level teaspoon caster sugar
6 tablespoons warm milk
1 level tablespoon dried yeast
8 oz (200 gm) plain flour
½ level teaspoon salt

4 standard eggs, fork-beaten
4 oz (100 gm) butter, melted

RUM SYRUP

4 oz (100 gm) granulated sugar
$\frac{1}{4}$ pint (125 ml) water
2 to 3 tablespoons rum
Juice of $\frac{1}{2}$ small lemon

1. Pre-heat oven to hot, 425°F or Gas No. 7 (218°C).
2. Brush 12 individual border or ring tins with melted butter. Stand on baking tray.
3. Dissolve sugar in the milk. Sprinkle yeast on top. Leave to stand in a warm place for about 20 to 25 minutes, or until frothy.
4. Sift flour and salt into mixer bowl. Add all remaining ingredients including yeast liquid.
5. Beat with beaters for 5 minutes.
6. Half-fill tins with Baba mixture.
7. Cover with a piece of greased polythene, and leave to rise until mixture reaches tops of tins.
8. Bake in centre of oven for 15 to 20 minutes.

Meanwhile make rum syrup

9. Dissolve sugar in the water without stirring.
10. Boil briskly for 5 minutes or until syrupy.
11. Remove from heat, and stir in rum and lemon juice.
12. Turn Babas out of tins and soak with rum syrup.
13. Leave until cold and, before serving, fill centres of each with whipped cream.

JAM DOUGHNUTS

Makes 10

1 level teaspoon caster sugar
2 tablespoons warm water
1 level dessertspoon dried yeast
8 oz (200 gm) plain flour
$\frac{1}{2}$ level teaspoon salt
1 oz (25 gm) lard or cooking fat
4 tablespoons warm milk
1 standard egg, fork-beaten
Red jam
Deep fat or oil for frying

COATING

5 level tablespoons caster sugar

1. Dissolve sugar in the water and sprinkle yeast on top. Leave to stand in a warm place for 10 to 15 minutes, or until frothy.
2. Sift flour and salt into bowl.
3. Rub in lard or cooking fat finely.
4. Add yeast liquid, warm milk, and egg.
5. Mix to dough with dough hook, then continue to knead with hook until dough is smooth and elastic.
6. Cover with a piece of greased polythene and leave to rise in a warm place for about 1 hour, or until dough has doubled in size and springs back when pressed lightly with the finger.
7. Uncover and knead lightly with hook until firm.
8. Divide into 10 equal-sized pieces.
9. Shape each into a ball, then press a hole in each with the thumb.
10. Fill with a little jam, then pinch up edges of dough so that jam is completely enclosed.
11. Cover with polythene, and leave to rise again in a warm place for 30 minutes.
12. Heat fat or oil until a cube of bread, dropped into it, will brown in 1 minute.
13. Fry doughnuts, a few at a time, for about 5 minutes.
14. Drain on paper towels, then roll in sugar.
15. Make and eat on same day.

85

CHAPTER 5

Drinks & Party Food

Milk and yogurt fruit shakes, ice cream sodas, iced coffee and chocolate, fruit floats, nogs, and vegetable juice cocktails are some of the mouth-watering blender drinks to be found in this section. All take seconds to make and all taste as good as they sound. Other blender and mixer recipes are designed for large and small get-togethers, and include a variety of dips, and hot and cold savoury snacks.

Drinks

NECTAR

Serves 1 to 2

½ pint (250 ml) canned, frozen or fresh orange juice, well-chilled
¼ pint (125 ml) natural yogurt
1 fresh peach, peeled, stoned and quartered

1. Put all ingredients into blender and blend until smooth.
2. Pour into one or two glasses.

ADAM'N'EVE

Serves 1

1 medium eating apple, washed and cored
Juice of ½ lemon
1 dessertspoon clear honey
¼ pint (125 ml) apple juice, well-chilled

1. Cut apple into eighths.
2. Put into blender with all remaining ingredients.
3. Blend until smooth.
4. Pour into glass. If liked, add one or two ice cubes.

CHOCOLATE MILK SHAKE

Serves 1

1 level tablespoon drinking chocolate
3 tablespoons boiling water
½ pint (250 ml) cold milk

1. Mix drinking chocolate and boiling water well together. Pour into blender.
2. Add milk and blend until smooth and frothy.
3. Pour into a glass and serve straight away.

SUNSET

Serves 2

½ pint (250 ml) canned pineapple juice, well-chilled
1 dessertspoon rose hip syrup
1 medium banana
1 heaped tablespoon vanilla ice cream
¼ pint (125 ml) milk, well-chilled

1. Put pineapple juice and rose hip syrup into blender.
2. Break banana into chunks, and add to blender with ice cream and milk.
3. Blend until smooth.
4. Pour into two glasses and serve straight away.

PEPPERMINT COOLER

Serves 1

1 heaped tablespoon vanilla ice cream
1 dessertspoon Crême de Menthe liqueur
¼ pint (125 ml) milk, well-chilled
Soda water or bitter lemon
Mint leaves

1. Put ice cream, liqueur, and milk into blender. Blend until smooth.
2. Pour into large tumbler, and top up with soda water or bitter lemon.
3. Float a few mint leaves on top.

BLACKCURRANT FROTH

Serves 2

2 tablespoons bottled blackcurrant syrup
½ pint (250 ml) buttermilk, well-chilled
2 heaped tablespoons vanilla ice cream
Bitter lemon

1. Put syrup, buttermilk and ice cream into blender. Blend until smooth.
2. Pour into two glasses and top up with bitter lemon.
3. Serve straight away.

ICED COFFEE

Serves 2

**2 heaped teaspoons instant coffee
granules or powder**
1 tablespoon boiling water
½ pint (250 ml) milk, well-chilled
**2 heaped tablespoons vanilla ice
cream**
**2 heaped teaspoons softly
whipped cream**
Cinnamon (optional)

1. Dissolve coffee in the boiling water.
2. Pour into blender. Add milk and
   ice cream, and blend until smooth
   and foamy.
3. Pour into two glasses.
4. Top with cream and sprinkle with
   cinnamon, if used.
5. Serve straight away.

ICED CHOCOLATE

Serves 2

**1½ level tablespoons drinking
chocolate**
2 tablespoons boiling water
½ pint (250 ml) milk, well-chilled
**2 heaped tablespoons vanilla,
coffee or chocolate ice-cream**
**2 heaped teaspoons softly
whipped cream**

1. Mix drinking chocolate and boiling
   water well together.
2. Follow recipe for Iced Coffee.

APRICOT AND GINGER FLOATS

Serves 4

**1 small can (8 oz or 200 gm)
apricots**
1 tablespoon ginger wine
Soda water
**4 heaped tablespoons vanilla ice
cream**

1. Put apricots, with syrup from can,
   into blender.
2. Add ginger wine. Blend until
   smooth.
3. Pour into four glasses and three-
   quarters fill with soda water.
4. Add tablespoon of ice cream to
   each and serve straight away.

EGG NOG

Serves 2

¾ pint (375 ml) cold milk
2 standard eggs
**2 level tablespoons granulated
sugar**
1 teaspoon vanilla essence
Nutmeg

1. Put all ingredients, except nutmeg,
   into blender.
2. Blend until frothy.
3. Pour into two glasses and sprinkle
   with nutmeg.
4. Serve straight away.

LIME FRAPPÉ

Serves 3 to 4

2 tablespoons lime cordial
Juice of 2 large oranges
¼ pint (125 ml) natural yogurt
1 egg white
**1 level tablespoon granulated
sugar**
Soda water, well-chilled

1. Put cordial, orange juice, yogurt,
   egg white, and sugar into blender.
   Blend until smooth.
2. Pour into four medium-sized
   glasses.
3. Top up with soda water and serve
   straight away.

STRAWBERRY OR RASPBERRY MILK SHAKE

Serves 2

**4 oz (100 gm) strawberries or
raspberries**
½ pint (250 ml) milk, well-chilled
**1 heaped tablespoon vanilla or
strawberry ice cream**

1. Put all ingredients into blender and
   blend until smooth and fluffy.
2. Pour into glasses and serve straight
   away.

BANANA MILK SHAKE

Serves 1 to 2

Follow recipe for Strawberry Milk
Shake and substitute 1 ripe banana for
the berries, breaking it into chunks
before adding to blender.

TOMATO, CARROT, AND CELERY COCKTAIL

Serves 4

¾ pint (375 ml) tomato juice, well-chilled
2 medium carrots, sliced
2 medium celery stalks
1 to 2 teaspoons Worcestershire sauce
½ to 1 level teaspoons salt

1. Put tomato juice and carrots into blender.
2. Break each celery stalk into 6 pieces.
3. Add to blender with Worcestershire sauce and salt. Blend until smooth.
4. Pour into four wine glasses and serve straight away.

HEALTH COCKTAIL

Serves 4

¼ pint (125 ml) water, well-chilled
½ teacup parsley
4 large tomatoes, skinned and quartered
¼ cucumber, peeled
1 medium carrot, sliced
2 medium celery stalks
1 teaspoon Worcestershire sauce
Salt to taste

1. Put water and parsley into blender.
2. Cut cucumber and break celery into pieces.
3. Add vegetables to blender with Worcestershire sauce and salt to taste. Blend until smooth.
4. Pour into glasses. If liked, add an ice cube to each.

Party Appetizers

PRAWN TARTS

Makes 18

8 oz Cheese Pastry (page 63)

FILLING

8 oz (200 gm) peeled prawns
2 standard eggs
1 small can evaporated milk
1 level teaspoon dry mustard
¼ to ½ level teaspoon salt
Pinch of Cayenne pepper

1. Pre-heat oven to hot, 425°F or Gas No. 7 (218°C).
2. Roll out pastry thinly and cut into 18 rounds with 3½ inch (8.5 cm) biscuit cutter.
3. Use to line 18 deep bun tins.
4. Prick lightly with fork, and line each with square of aluminium foil to prevent pastry from rising as it cooks.
5. Bake near top of oven for 10 minutes.
6. Remove from oven and carefully lift out pieces of foil.

7. Reduce oven temperature to moderate, 350°F or Gas No. 4 (177°C).
8. Spoon equal amounts of prawns into each pastry-lined bun tin.
9. Put all remaining ingredients into blender. Run machine until smooth.
10. Pour into bun tins.
11. Return to oven and bake tarts for approximately 20 minutes, or until filling is set.
12. Serve hot.

cestershire sauce, and beaten egg. Mix together thoroughly.

4. Shape into 12 even-sized balls with damp hands.
5. Make a well in each by pressing in with thumb.
6. Press onions into wells and enclose by sealing sausagemeat round them.
7. Stand on greased baking tray and bake in centre of oven for 30 minutes.
8. Spear a cocktail stick into each and serve hot.

EGG, GREEN PEPPER, AND ONION DIP

Serves 8 to 12

$\frac{1}{2}$ small green pepper, diced
1 small onion, sliced
4 tablespoons Mayonnaise (page 36)
2 tablespoons natural yogurt
$\frac{1}{4}$ level teaspoon salt
$\frac{1}{2}$ teaspoon Worcestershire sauce
6 hard-boiled eggs, quartered
Paprika

1. Put all ingredients, except eggs and paprika, into blender.
2. Run machine until pepper and onion are both finely chopped.
3. Add eggs. Run machine until coarsely chopped.
4. Transfer to small dish and sprinkle with paprika.
5. Stand on platter, and surround with dips of carrot slices, savoury biscuits and 2 inch lengths of celery.

STUFFED PRUNES

Makes 12

1 dozen large prunes
4 oz (100 gm) Cheddar cheese, cubed
1 oz (25 gm) softened butter
Pinch of Cayenne pepper
$\frac{1}{4}$ level teaspoon prepared mustard
Mayonnaise (page 36)
1 dozen shelled walnut halves

1. Cover prunes with hot water and leave to soak for 3 to 4 hours.
2. Put cheese cubes, a few at a time,

TOMATO DIP

Serves 8 to 12

$\frac{1}{4}$ pint (125 ml) natural yogurt
$\frac{1}{4}$ pint (125 ml) double cream
1 teaspoon Worcestershire sauce
1 packet tomato soup (enough to make 1 pint or approximately $\frac{1}{2}$ litre)

1. Put all ingredients into blender. Run machine until smooth.
2. Transfer to bowl and chill 3 to 4 hours.
3. Spoon into small serving dish.
4. Stand on platter, and surround with small unsalted cocktail biscuits, slices of peeled cucumber and potato crisps.

PORK AND ONION NIBBLES

Makes 12

2 oz (50 gm) white bread, diced
8 oz (200 gm) pork sausagemeat
1 level teaspoon dry mustard
$\frac{1}{4}$ teaspoon Worcestershire sauce
1 standard egg, fork-beaten
12 cocktail onions, well-drained

1. Pre-heat oven to fairly hot, 400°F or Gas No. 6 (204°C).
2. Put bread dice, a few at a time, into blender. Run machine until bread is reduced to fine crumbs. Put into bowl.
3. Add sausagemeat, mustard, Wor-

into blender. Run machine until very finely chopped.

3. Beat butter with a fork until creamy. Gradually beat in cheese, Cayenne pepper, and mustard.
4. Stir in sufficient mayonnaise to make mixture thick and creamy.
5. Drain prunes and make a slit in each.
6. Remove stones, then fill prunes with cheese mixture.
7. Top each with a shelled walnut half and chill at least 1 hour before serving.

AVOCADO AND CELERY DIP

Serves 8 to 10

2 medium celery stalks, each broken into 4
1 small garlic clove
¼ pint (125 ml) soured cream
1 level teaspoon salt
Juice of ½ medium lemon
1 large avocado
Freshly milled black pepper

1. Put celery, garlic, cream, salt, and lemon juice into blender.
2. Peel avocado and cut flesh into chunks.
3. Add to blender. Run machine until celery and garlic are finely chopped.
4. Transfer to bowl and season with black pepper. Cover with foil and chill for 1 hour.
5. Spoon into small serving dish and stand on platter.
6. Surround with dips of savoury biscuits, small florets of cauliflower, and potato crisps.

SAUSAGES WITH CREAMY PIQUANT SAUCE

Serves 6 to 8

¼ pint (125 ml) double cream
1 level teaspoon caster sugar
1 tablespoon milk
1 tablespoon bottled horseradish sauce
1 level teaspoon paprika
¼ level teaspoon salt
1 level teaspoon prepared mustard
1 lb (approximately ½ kilo) freshly grilled or fried cocktail sausages

1. Put cream into mixer bowl with sugar and milk. With mixer at low speed, beat with beaters until thick.
2. Stir in horseradish sauce, paprika, salt, and prepared mustard.
3. Mix thoroughly and spoon into small serving bowl.
4. Stand on platter and surround with hot sausages.

CREAM CHEESE AND OLIVE SAVOURIES

Serves about 6

1 packet (3 oz or 75 gm) cream cheese, cubed
3 tablespoons single cream
½ small green pepper, diced
¼ level teaspoon salt
1 level teaspoon canned or tubed tomato purée
Buttered cocktail biscuits
Stuffed olives, sliced

1. Put cheese cubes into blender with cream, green pepper, salt and tomato purée.
2. Run machine until mixture is smooth and pepper is fairly finely chopped.
3. Spread on biscuits and top each with a slice of olive.

DEVILLED CHICKEN AND EGG FINGERS

Serves about 8

3 tablespoons Mayonnaise (page 36)
1 small onion, sliced
1 teaspoon Worcestershire sauce
Large pinch of Cayenne pepper
1 level tablespoon sweet pickle
4 oz (100 gm) cold cooked chicken, diced
2 hard-boiled eggs, quartered
Fingers of hot buttered toast

1. Put mayonnaise, onion, Worcestershire sauce, Cayenne pepper, and sweet pickle into blender.
2. Blend until onion is finely chopped.
3. Add chicken and eggs. Blend until both are finely chopped.
4. Spread on fingers of hot buttered toast.

CHAPTER 6

Dishes for Baby

When your baby begins to take solid food, the great advantage of having a blender is that all sorts of tasty meals can be made quickly, easily and economically from part of the meat, vegetable and dessert dishes being prepared for the rest of the family.

This automatically gives baby an opportunity of getting used to 'Mum's cooking' from an early age, and at the same time enables Mum to introduce plenty of variety and imagination into baby's diet.

Here are some suggestions for main dishes and desserts.

LIVER AND BACON DINNER

1 oz (25 gm) cooked liver, diced
1 lean bacon rasher, cooked and
  diced
1 rounded tablespoon mashed
  potato
3 tablespoons thin gravy

1. Put all ingredients into blender.
2. Run machine at high speed for
   about 2 minutes, or until ingredients
   are chopped finely enough for baby.
3. Transfer to saucepan and simmer
   gently for 10 minutes, stirring
   frequently.
4. Season with a little salt if necessary.

STEWED BEEF AND VEGETABLE DINNER

1 oz (25 gm) stewed beef
1 heaped tablespoon vegetables
  from stew
1 level tablespoon mashed
  potato
3 tablespoons gravy from stew

Follow method for Liver and Bacon
Dinner.

LAMB, GREEN PEA, AND MACARONI DINNER

1 oz (25 gm) cooked lamb, diced
1 heaped tablespoon cooked peas
1 rounded tablespoon cooked
  macaroni
3 tablespoons thin gravy

Follow method for Liver and Bacon
Dinner.

CREAMED SMOKED HADDOCK DINNER

1½ oz (37 gm) cooked smoked
  haddock, with all skin and
  bones removed
1 rounded tablespoon mashed
  potato
1 small parsley sprig
4 tablespoons milk
1 egg yolk

1. Put all ingredients except egg
   yolk into blender.
2. Run machine at high speed for
   2 minutes, or until ingredients are
   finely chopped and mixture is
   smooth.
3. Transfer to saucepan and heat
   through gently for about 5 minutes,
   stirring frequently.
4. Remove from heat and stir in egg
   yolk.
5. Season with a little salt if necessary.

CHICKEN AND CARROT DINNER

1 oz (25 gm) cold cooked chicken,
  diced
1 cooked carrot, sliced
½ cooked potato, diced
3 tablespoons water
1 egg yolk
¼ level teaspoon yeast extract (or
  less according to taste)

1. Put chicken, carrot, potato, and
   water into blender.
2. Run machine at high speed for
   about 2 minutes, or until ingredients
   are chopped finely enough for baby.
3. Transfer to saucepan and simmer
   gently for 10 minutes, stirring
   frequently.
4. Remove from heat, and stir in egg
   yolk and yeast extract.
5. Season with a little salt if necessary.

BEEF, TOMATO, AND RICE DINNER

1 oz (25 gm) cold cooked beef,
  diced
1 small tomato, skinned and
  quartered
1 rounded tablespoon boiled rice
1 very thin slice of onion
3 tablespoons water
¼ level teaspoon yeast extract (or
  less according to taste)

1. Put all ingredients except yeast
   extract into blender.
2. Run machine at high speed for
   about 2 minutes, or until ingredients
   are chopped finely enough for baby.
3. Transfer to saucepan and simmer
   gently for 10 minutes, stirring
   frequently.
4. Remove from heat and stir in yeast
   extract.
5. Season with a little salt if necessary.

VEAL AND MIXED VEGETABLE DINNER

1 oz (25 gm) cooked veal, diced
1 heaped tablespoon cooked mixed vegetables
1 very thin slice of onion
1 small parsley sprig
1 level teaspoon semolina
4 tablespoons tomato juice
Pinch of sugar
¼ level teaspoon yeast extract (or less according to taste)

Follow method for Beef, Tomato, and Rice Dinner (page 93).

IRISH STEW AND TOMATO DINNER

1 oz (25 gm) stewed lamb, all fat removed
1 heaped tablespoon vegetables from stew
1 small tomato, skinned and quartered
3 tablespoons water
¼ level teaspoon yeast extract (or less according to taste)

Follow method for Beef, Tomato, and Rice Dinner (page 93).

APPLE HONEY

2 tablespoons stewed apples
2 tablespoons custard
1 to 2 level teaspoons clear honey

1. Put all ingredients into blender. Blend until smooth.
2. If liked, warm through before giving to baby.

TUTTI FRUTTI DESSERT

2 canned apricot halves
½ medium banana

2 level teaspoons honey
Juice of ½ small orange

Follow method for Apple Honey.

SEMOLINA AND PRUNE DESSERT

3 tablespoons cooked semolina pudding
4 canned or stewed prunes, stoned
2 tablespoons prune juice

Follow method for Apple Honey.

RICE AND PEAR DESSERT

3 tablespoons canned or home-made rice pudding
1 canned pear half, quartered
1 teaspoon plum jam
2 teaspoons pear syrup

Follow method for Apple Honey.

BANANA CUSTARD

1 small banana
2 tablespoons custard
2 teaspoons rose hip syrup

1. Break banana into chunks.
2. Put into blender with remaining ingredients.
3. Run machine at high speed until smooth.
4. Give to baby cold.

PEACH YOGURT

3 tablespoons natural yogurt
1 canned peach half, quartered
2 teaspoons rose hip or blackcurrant syrup

1. Put all ingredients into blender.
2. Blend until smooth.
3. Give to baby cold.

INDEX

95